AF522486

THE SIN OF OMISSION

MOHD. FAIZAN

Invincible Publishers

First published in India in 2019

ISBN : 978-93-88333-76-4

Invincible Publishers

Registered Address: 201A, SAS Tower, Sector 38, Gurgaon-122003

Printed in India by Excel Printers Pvt. Ltd.

Dedicated to my mother Rehnuma Khatoon,

the perfect combination of a strong and gentle soul who taught me to have unshakable belief in the Almighty Allah,

and relentlessly encouraged me to work harder towards my goals.

I shall always be indebted to her.

Acknowledgement

First and foremost, many thanks to Ammi who's been instrumental in making this book possible. My siblings, Nusrat and Farhan, who goaded on me to never give up, particularly when I was hedged in by a score of responsibilities and had virtually decided to let it go. Of course, Mr. Nek Mohammad (Professor of English), who infused in me a remarkable orientation towards the English language. Your help and encouragement mean a great deal. Thank you very much!

Mr. Mukseh Sharma (eminent lawyer, teacher and writer) who ceaselessly motivated me to think big. He once said, "Faizan, aim for the moon." Thank you for all your advice.

Not to miss a mighty name, Mr. Ajay Setia (Director, Invincible Publishers), who approved of my manuscript and graciously gave a way to publish this work. Thanks a ton! Thanks to my editor Aditi Saxena and designer Ashish Samant for giving the book the form that it has today. Mohd. Kashif, my alter ego and partner in crime, you've phenomenally helped me in pulling me out of my sorrows and agony by your humour. Thanks in plenty.

Lastly, my wife Zainab Parveen – you're completely irreplaceable in my life. Thank you for everything and I hope you like the book.

Table of Contents

My Silly Dream

"Good afternoon! My name is Mohd. Zaid. I am a graduate in English literature from Delhi

University and have a Post Graduate Diploma in Business Management. I started my career as a Customer Service Associate at Vodafone when I was still in my first year of graduation. After that, I worked as an Investment Adviser at a brokerage house, named Shri Ram Insight Shares Broker Limited. Then, I went to work for the UK Education Department of British Council on a temporary basis. After completing graduation, I decided to go for a professional qualification and completed PGDM with specialization in Human Resource and Marketing. Currently, I am working as a freelance content writer based out of Delhi and I create content for websites, articles, forums, blogs, etc. As a SEO expert, I have contributed to several websites of different domains, like ad agencies, website designing firms, lifestyle portals dealing with topics of health, food, fashion, travel, home, self-help, pets, etc. I have composed many poems and am also writing a book, which will be published soon. I have my own website too by the name of Zaid Rajput."

"Very nice! So, Mr. Mohd. Zaid, is that all about you?" Anchal Khanna, my interviewer from Times of India asked further.

"Yes, ma'am. Have you shortlisted me for the content writer's post?" I enquired, emphasizing particularly on *me*.

Dear reader, it was a futile dream.

My mother announced her first morning slogan, "Zaid... Zaid...Zaid, it's 6.40 AM already. You will miss the *fajar namaaz* (morning prayer) again, as usual. Don't take too long to change!" This is how my professional dream splintered into pieces, as it had already happened several times in my childhood.

Even though I heard her say it all, it felt as if *Ammi* had commanded me in my dream, or it was all déjà vu. Anyway, I resuscitated myself quickly and conveyed my traditional *salaam* (greetings) to her. A pair of Islamic attires was hanging on pegs for me. I swiftly changed into them, skipping the call of nature too, while at it. I rushed to the *masjid* and was fortunately able to join the prayer in time.

Here, I must mention the effect of *wuzu* (ablution) which rejuvenates the worshippers magically; I could feel that much-needed freshness entering into me. It had barely been a year or so since I had successfully completed my *madarsa taaleem* (Islamic education). Customarily, I was encouraged to study the Holy Quran along with basic Islamic jurisprudence. Out of the numerous students, I had topped the chart in terms of brilliance. After I was certified by Jamia Arabia Taleem-Ul-Islam, Dasna (Hapur), my *Dada ji* got me back to Delhi for better academic prospects. By and large, I was a blank page with no writer intending to fill in.

While coming back home from the mosque that morning, I witnessed a road accident. A Santro car had banged into a police booth, resulting in three casualties. 'Nearer the church, farther from God,' I reserved in my mind. A large group of school going kids could be seen on the spot. Illumination, eagerness and adventure could be monitored in their eyes, as it used to be in ours when we admired *Shaktimaan* (an Indian superhero TV periodic). I geared up to participate in the customary action.

"Off the car! Off the car!" a senior policeman shouted at the kids. His unshaven, unkempt look made him resemble Nana Patekar, the actor. I could guess the reason behind his grumpy voice – perhaps he hadn't had his free cup of tea and butter omelet from the road side vendors.

"Oh! The driver of the car is in police uniform and is miserably wounded," an elderly man revealed aloud, fluttering his anxious eyes.

"How is it possible for a policeman to hit another policemen?" I questioned the kids curiously.

"Anything can happen on this road." a kid answered smartly, but looked rather grim.

"Is there something inauspicious about this road?" I poked again. There was no response this time. Perhaps my question made no sense to the onlookers. Moreover, the timing was not appropriate to get answers to such pesky questions. A few minutes passed in dead silence. We soon learnt that the driver in the police uniform was a sub inspector. He was rushed to the nearby dispensary, more out of the initiative taken by the crowd than the other policemen, who had been unable to arrive at a remedial decision in that moment. The rest of the unproductive crowd was dispersed off by a booth officer.

I rushed back home to get ready for school. They say that distance lends to enchantment, but my school was unfortunately only at a walking distance from my house. Consequently, I found myself quite distant academically. My school uniform was no less than that of a member of a wedding band in the city. The brown trousers and white shirt were entirely typical and distinctive of my learning temple 'Shafiq Memorial Senior Secondary School' in the whole city.

"I've put your breakfast in the other room, finish it before you leave," *Ammi* ordered frowningly. Her anger was completely justified as I had already gotten too late for school. As I mentioned earlier, I took my academics for granted and the reason was convenience. I devoured the Britannia toasted bread, simultaneously gulping down a large mug of tea.

It had been exactly three days since I had bathed. This time, I splashed water on my face and sprinkled some over my hair through a water bottle. I left home around

7.30 PM, even though the school started at 7:15 sharp. It was mandatory to wear neat and proper uniform along with a tie which, as a matter of fact, never existed in the dictionary of my classmates. Hence, I never bothered to appear as a proper school going boy, partly because of my resistance to change and partly my useless mind which dictated, "Why should I study?"

When I reached my school, I saw the class already in session and realised that I had almost entirely missed the first period of science. I was caught by Mr. Saeed who hailed me belligerently. "Zaid, please come here, sir." I was fourteen and had no interest even in basic Mathematics. My teachers disliked me for my obtrusive absenteeism. There were a total of forty five students in my class, but the daily attendance never rose above twenty four. Surprisingly, such a statistic was religiously maintained by the entire school. The endeavors of our government went all in vain, for none of us seemed particularly sincere on a personal level.

Due to an inferiority complex and my parents' unfair expectations from an empty head like me, my aspirations always appeared unattainable to myself. I knew nothing about jobs, duties or services. Actually, by the grace of God, I always had deep confidence in attempting questions, but never thought beyond that. Hence, I was never able to score high enough. The question, 'Why should I study?' had settled itself inside my mind. Despite having grown up to be a teenager, my grasping power was worse than a primary schooler.

"I would like to welcome you for your punctuality and dedication," said Mr. Saeed sarcastically.

All the students frowned at Mr. Saeed since they were not very happy with him either.

I knew that they all were chips of my lot too. Mr. Saeed always pretended to deliver speeches as seriously as Dr. Abdul Kalam while visiting various universities as chief speaker, but he always failed to ape his style. Hence, his words had no impact on me. Even though I dreamed of flying high, keeping pace with the world, my actions never fell in the right direction. There was no one to direct or guide me regarding building a career. All I cared about was enjoying each moment to the fullest, whether at home, at school, or while travelling between these two places.

After welcoming me, he grabbed my hand and pulled me inside the classroom, like a sheep dragged on by the shepherd, then immediately launched a volley of admonitions at me. "Your exams are approaching. They are just three months away, and you are still not sincere about it even a bit. Have you ever thought of moving ahead in life? Can't you learn from the eagles who start accumulating food for themselves and their eaglets before the rainy season sets in? You are fortunate enough that you need not support any eaglets or children yet. It's just you and your life that you need to take responsibility for, Zaid," he vented.

He paused then for a minute or so to catch his breath, perhaps marveling at his own humor

I somehow stomached his period, then skipped the next three in order to successfully compensate at a stretch. As usual, I managed to leave the school premises before 1 PM. It was the peon who always proved his loyalty towards us seasoned bribers who had the gates opened early by greasing his palms with a paltry amount. It had gotten ingrained in my system not to stay at school for more than three hours, occasionally four when a sports trial happened or a special guest was invited, since we all received refreshments at such events.

I arrived home at exactly 1:15 PM. It was a routine for me to reach our residence before half past one at noon to share a delicious lunch with my lovely mother. She was the only creature on earth whose face, consolation and scolding all comforted me equally. Even if she rushed after me for my careless attitude regarding school, I never had that loathing in my eyes that many other insensitive and boorish boys my age did. I always held *Ammi* in great respect, as it was she who always prayed for us whenever we were away from home for a taxing work. It was also miraculous that whatever she implored Allah for us, she got granted most definitely. It had been a part of my maternal grandfather's bringing-up that my *Ammi* was conditioned for, that whenever she begged before Allah for something, it was always for others, instead of her own preservation.

When I arrived home, *Ammi* came to me and asked with a gloomy face, "My son, would you like to see your mother's crowned head hanging low in shame because of your wretched annual mark sheet?"

Looked like Mr. Saeed had called home to tell my *Ammi* how sincere he was being with me, telling her my marks and routine as diligently as if he cared the most for me.

It wsan't new for her. My mother was all too aware of my insincere attitude towards studies. And it was not the first time she had come to me to reason with me to study better and be a better student altogether but this time when she said it, her face held a moroseness that I had never witnessed before. It took me aback and my mother's seemingly simple and small words held great power over my heart. My mother had, on this day, engraved an indelible motto in my mind that I had to succeed without looking back upon my obscurities from the past.

I replied to my *Ammi* optimistically, "*Ammi* jaan, your son will never let your shining face down. I will qualify with flying colors." She appreciated this promising spirit in me.

The very next morning, I reached school on time. My class teacher, Mr. Hamid Sheikh, saw me attend the morning assembly for the first time in as long as he had known me. "I welcome this reformed version of you," he said.

"Sir, where there's a will, there's a way." I replied candidly. He just smiled this time.

Once the prayers got over, the herd of students were rushed back to their respective classes. I headed towards my destination too, room #12 which was my classroom. I grabbed the front desk, as opposed to the last one, which was my usual. I took out my science book the same moment Mr. Saeed Ahmad, who also taught us science, entered and received our sing song greetings of 'Good morning, sir' with a gruff voice. He asked us to open our books to page number 48, lesson number six.

While fiddling through the pages of his file, he looked up to catch a single glance of the class, and fortunately captured my presence on the first bench. It struck him at once, and he looked at me somewhat surprised. Without any argument however, he had to concede that it was indeed me, Zaid–the reformed student.

It was not only Mr. Saeed who noticed my changed and sincere appearance that day, but all the other teachers too who were acquainted with me. I had been infamous for my daily tussles with everyone at school. What can I say? My learning temple was founded in a barbaric locality, the sort where people actively engaged in hooliganism. They considered school education quite worthless. The students of my class hence had their behaviour conditioned by this very kind of attitude that they had grown up seeing. Bullying was commonplace within the school premises. But I was not one of those cowards who swallowed the unreasonable attitude of those depraved boys. In sober words, I put a curb on their unrestricted tyranny over the other students.

I was the paramount personality of my group, as it was I alone who could (and had) thwart anyone's blow against myself or my friends.

It was the first time in my life when I was attending a class most seriously and wholeheartedly. I did not skip the next three periods either and remained seated at my desk until the bell rang for recess. I felt really relieved and light as a sparrow after having studied honestly for so long. My friends had gestured at me to bunk with them during the second and third period, but I had evaded them

When my friends came to know about this latest commitment of mine, they could not refrain from coaxing me out of it. One of my closest ones, Rafeeq Shah, approached me during the lunch break at the canteen, crouched over me like a lion over a lamb, and blurted out with a concerned face, "Zaid, what a disgusting attitude you are displaying today! You have not taken the least bit of interest in our daily hangouts. May I know which poor beam of sunshine has infused this curiosity for learning in your insincere soul?"

At first, I nudged him away from my seat, then replied, "I am still capricious, but a civilized one," which was enough to sew his lips into silence. Then, I left the canteen and spent the rest of my time in the classroom, studying with a focused-mind.

It was the first time in my life when I reached home at 1:45, having attended all the classes sincerely. I adorned this attitude from that day that I would never bunk. When our exams were just about twenty days away, one of my teachers, Mr. Kalaam, announced loudly in class, "I want to foretell the result of some students here who I know won't get through 10th standard."

I knew that my name would be the first in his stupid prediction, and so it was indeed.

"Dear Zaid," he continued. "You alone will receive the worst marks in the final result. I'd be surprised if you score any more than 30/100 in even a single subject.

Does anybody have anything to say?" he asked further to the class in general.

Before anyone could come with a query, I stood up immediately and told him, "Sir, my mark sheet will better speak for me."

That day, I got another challenge from my uncle, Mr. Mohd. Rizwan. I was standing at a coffee shop in the evening on Saturday, when his boorish gaze fell upon me while he was passing by it, and I became his all- time favorite casualty. He approached me and started upbraiding me right there amidst a huge crowd. He never left any chance to humiliate me by launching into a prolonged sermon, whenever he caught me at some shop with my friends. This day was particularly the worst, as he said, "Zaid, you can never study in your life. You are simply letting all my brother's endeavors go to waste."

The words inflamed my soul because *Abbu* had never paid an attentive eye to me. He was always either beating me, admonishing me or insulting me, as if I was his adopted or illegitimate son. It was *Ammi* who tried to placate me after I had been taken to task by *Abbu*. While I got a beating, *Ammi* had no right to defend me or speak a single word to exonerate me. She had to swallow this tyrannical behavior from *Abbu* without raising any objection.

I did not respond to my uncle, and pursed my lips to hold my silence. I rushed back home soon after and splashed some water on my face, asking myself, "Zaid, are you only to receive embarrassment from your elders?" I was aggrieved to such an extent that I decided not to come out of my room until my exams began. I limited myself to remain within my house and studied harder. I was determined to give a crisp answer to all the long tirades of pesky relatives and teachers. I found trigonometry a bit tough, yet I learnt its logics so that I would not miss out on scoring from those questions. I had not had any tutor throughout the year.

Finally, the third of March arrived, the day of my first exam. I was fully prepared to purge out on the answer sheets whatever I had crammed during the previous month. After breakfast, *Ammi* came to me to give me her blessings. *Ammi*'s blessings always invoked an intellectually noble spirit in me, but this comfort was only momentary. My father, who always castigated me for something or the other, came to me and conferred a hefty slap on my cheek. I was completely stunned for a while, not able to understand what I had done to deserve such a smacking.

My mother rushed into the room, suspecting that something awful had taken place. When she took measure of the scene, she didn't waste even a single moment to apprehend what had been done to me. *Ammi* questioned *Abbu* on his insensitivity, that too on the day of my exam. He replied, "I've come to know that he listens to songs in the street during noon, when he should remain at home for the sake of his studies. All the money that I have spent over his stupid education..." A sudden hiccup stopped him from continuing.

I could not speak up to defend myself at that moment.

After having given me the bitterest version of his blessings, Abbu left for office. My mother came to console me and uplifted my mood into a pleasant state as before. I soon left my house to go sit for the exam, but my mind was tumultuous with the thought of how I was taken by everyone and what they thought of me. Was I not worth my father's love and care, his own biological son? At that precise moment, a sense of determination flared in my heart that I would do anything to out-do *Abbu* in earning both name and fame. These words got engraved on my heart in the ink of cold blood that could never be blotched off.

Ramit's Coaching

Three months passed by in a blur as I waited for my results. I had complete hope of getting through with average marks and I was content with that. Actually, I always believed in learning heuristically as it led to self-control and independence, both of which I needed to continue my life as it was. More so because I had never even dreamt of getting any blessings or help from my Abbu, be it monetary or emotional. I was occupied with similar thoughts that day when I heard the telephone on the table ringing. I received the call to hear my friend Anas Jafar on the other side.

"Hey, Zaid!" he started. "Are you lost or what? Our results have been declared. I've got wretched marks, but at least I have passed. How did you score, dude? You might have got pathetic marks, I guess!" He blurted out in a single breath. I terminated the call right away and requested *Ammi* to sink in supplication for my good result. I donned my kurta and stepped out of the house in search of the nearest cyber café. Before I left, *Ammi* comforted and pacified me, despite the presence of the conspicuous monster in the house, *Abbu*.

When I reached the café, I found nobody else there, besides the shop owner and the computer operator. I was either too early or too late to get my result. I shared

my roll number with the computer operator who fiddled with the keyboard for the next ten minutes. With the anxiety and annoyance growing within me, I slapped his head from behind.

"Mr. Zaid, I am trying to get what you want, but you are doubling my stress," he complained, rubbing the back of his head lightly. I remained silent, but mocked inwardly his stressful occupation. After about ten more minutes, as my destiny and I waited eagerly, my result page popped up on the screen. The intense anticipation had blurred my vision and I only read the last line in bold and the word that shone at the end, PASSED. My exultant heart found a voice as I bellowed out my unrestrained joy. I recalled how I had always been spurned by *Abbu,* my teachers and friends, and how all of them had been proved wrong! Only my *Ammi* had consoled and encouraged me each time that I could do even the most strenuous and taxing tasks. My joyful exclamations filled and reverberated through the tiny space of the cyber café.

My happiness was so exhilarating that I did not even bother to look at my marks. I only knew that I had gotten through. I met my friends on the way, and seeing my pearly smile, they speculated that I had cleared all the subjects. They demanded *Nahari roti* as a treat from me and grabbed me so I wouldn't be able to escape. But I managed to break free of them somehow, and rushed straight home to my *Ammi* who was still in *Jaye namaz,* praying hard for me. I screamed loudly, "*Ammi* jaan! I made it, I made it, I made it, I made it, I made it!!"

I uttered this greatest moment of my slim academic career five times, perhaps because I had five subjects and I wanted to sound it out for each one of them, as if it wouldn't be real if I didn't say it. My *Ammi* had tears rolling down her cheeks as she blessed me and hugged me warmly. I felt as if I had attained paradise to relax in.

At that very next moment, my Abbu emerged from his room, yawning like a giant. His hair was all dishevelled, quite resembling an eagle's nest. Intoxicated with the joy of my happy result, I approached him in a rejoicing mood and said, "Abbu ji, I passed all my exams."

No flash of even a smile flitted across his face, and contrary to how I had expected him to respond, he enquired like the villain Gabbar from the movie Sholey, "How much did you score?"

He frowned at me, sitting cross-legged on a rocking chair before me. I was in as pitiable a condition as was Dilip Kumar in Ganga Jamuna on being wrongfully accused of robbery and brought to the court for investigation. I replied, "Abbu, umm…I think it was around 60 or 55%."

When he did not look pleased, I corrected myself saying, "No! No! I remember the screen now, it was exactly 65%."

This was my feeble trial to escape from that quandary that I suddenly found myself in. The news must have rubbed him the wrong way, for he picked up his cell phone the very next moment and pressed a key to call my uncle Rizwan, whom he considered as the most intellectual man. My father consulted my uncle on everything, even whether it would be better for him to take water before his meals or after.

"It's Farooq," he started. "I have to make sure what percentage Zaid should have got in his exams. Tell me quickly."

"I think, it must be above 65% or so," reported my uncle. It seemed to me that my Abbu had made this call only to justify acting on his boorish desire of hitting me black and blue, since I had not gotten marks according to my uncle. "Rizwan is coming here to inspect your progress," said my Abbu sternly after terminating the call. In about ten minutes, my uncle arrived ready with his thoroughly critical remarks. When he approached me and asked about my result, I gave him the same reply that I had given my *Abbu*. My uncle, who was no less of a wild creature than *Abbu*, gave a tremendous reward of all my toil.

"It would have been far better had you flunked your exams altogether. Even though, no nephew of ours has ever cleared class 10th yet, you have brought us heavy shame by getting through with such pathetic marks," he blasted. "Pity be on you, you dope!"

My eyes turned red with boiling rage, but I curbed my anger somehow, thinking of my *Ammi*. I knew that my *Ammi* would be denounced by everyone in the community and face the brunt of their beratement if I committed an act of scorn against any of my elders. I rushed out of the house and spent almost the next three hours pondering over my childhood and all the nostalgic affairs of my life. I hadn't had a morsel of food all morning. Spending a good amount of time on the street all alone did not come as a difficult challenge for me, since there was no paucity of bland moments that remained to be remembered and cursed. The perennial question in my mind was, "Why is it only me who is criticized, targeted and handed out humiliation by *Abbu*?" It was a day of celebration for me, yet I was to mourn because of my father's upbraiding.

Filled with regret for having got such a father, tremendous anger coursed through me the very next moment and I got down from the scooty I was sitting on. I tightened my fists and grounded my teeth for the next few minutes, as it was the perfect time and avenue for me to purge out my anger. I opened my eyes as a pretty idea struck my mind. I decided to spend the rest of my time partying with my friends. I had already wasted away enough time contemplating the reaction of someone as inconsequential as *Abbu* who had never before laid an attentive eye on me. I got to my friend's house and we planned to throw a big party together. We decided to have only the best meat served for food there and even invited a local DJ to play for us. I rejoiced to my heart's brim as I had no sign of sorrow left in me anymore.

Since nobody from my family was present there, I rested assured that our fun would not get spoiled. We were all feasting on roasted chicken when one of my friends broached the topic of what we would choose as our subject in class 11th. "I suggest we take up science so that we can produce a master chemical that has the power to change all our stoic parents into permissive ones," Sameer said. His amusing idea made us all laugh hysterically. Another guy prompted that we should take humanities since it was the easiest. At last, I shared my own two penny by suggesting that we take commerce since it would cultivate our minds for business and the accounting sector. I could visualize myself in the future tackling every hardship with my knowledge of commerce and took delight in it.

Around seven in the evening, we returned all that we had used at my friend's house to its former position and fixed up my friend's room where we had been enjoying. His mother was about to arrive soon, and he would have had to listen to her music had we not set everything in order. I bid farewell to my chums and reached back home. It had become a part of my daily routine that I had to be home by seven in the evening, before my father arrived, come hell or high water. Such was the terror of my Abbu. I had eaten so much at the party that I was full up to my neck when I got back home. My *Ammi,* my divine light indeed, served me delicious chicken and I did not lose even a single moment to thank her for the treat on the occasion of my good result.

I was to join back at school after a month and had made up my mind about my choice of stream. I was the eldest of my siblings, so I was on my own to think and decide the best subjects that could be dealt with smoothly. I got my name enrolled for commerce, but without mathematics because it was the real beast among all the subjects. I was preparing myself to attend my first accountancy class, feeling both apprehensive and excited, when I came across another teacher, Mr. Atir Rao, who taught Economics. Upon seeing me, he grew that surprised look on his face as if he had not expected to see me at school after the class X board exams. "Dear Zaid, how nice to see you again!" he exclaimed, then continued, "You must not go for Economics at all, because you don't have the potential required to accomplish such a complicated subject."

I appraised the delicacy of time since I had been thrown a challenge, the kind that I had now developed a penchant for accepting. "Dear sir, it may be somewhat pathetic for you to have me as your student right from this memorable moment, but I love studying taxonomic affairs in economics as well as statistics," I retorted.

Upon getting rid of him, I started attending my classes on a regular basis, barring Fridays and Saturdays. I had grown decently sophisticated by now and had set myself on the right track. It was the spell of my *Ammi* who ceaselessly prayed for me not to be led astray in any circumstance. It was another matter that I still continued hanging out with my friends at least thrice a month or more. Regardless, I remained fully conscious that I had to clear the years to follow without a fall. A catastrophic feeling always hung over my head like a sword, threatening to chop me into tiny pieces if I ever disappointed my father.

My class tests were going well, but I was facing challenges in accountancy, so I decided to join some coaching and got myself admitted to a nearby coaching center. The tutor was known to all the near-by school going children as arrogant and a bit conceited, and I was ignored by him big time! My tutor was Mr. Ramit Goel who declared after only a week, "Zaid, I envisage that you will never be able to attain any goal because of your narrow caliber. You cannot capture the tactics of accountancy."

I did not respond to him as I was occupied at that time making calculations for a balance sheet question given in D.K. Goyal's book of Accountancy. He was actually prejudiced against me, as I was informed by one of the girls at the same coaching, and always held a foul opinion of me, so I decided to break up with that center and study on my own. Initially after leaving his coaching, I faced some challenges and confusion with the practical subjects, but soon recovered and got acquainted with all topics with ease.

First Day in Mundka

2 years later

It was the 14th of May, my 12th class board results had been declared just that morning and I had passed with flying colours. With an aggregate percentage of 79.6%, my result shone compatible to all the hard work that I had put in. A special mention needs to be made here of this fortunate occasion since I was not at the receiving end of any caustic remarks from my father or my paternal relatives. This was bound to happen because a cousin of mine who had been studying with me in class 12th had flunked the same year. By God's grace, I even received appreciation by my grandpa. My father was only a puppet who did what he saw his parents do, and smiled accordingly. I was advised by my grandpa to take up B.Com for my graduate study. However, this was not to be the end of my troubles and I could not hope to ascend with such ease. Soon after, there popped up the uninvited obstacle of my age. When I had first taken admission at my school, my grandpa had gotten my age written a year lesser than my real one in my birth certificate so I would never fall behind other kids in my educational pursuits. Ironically, this became the barrier for me as I was rendered ineligible for a graduate course in any university.

I remained insipid for two consecutive days and wished that I had better failed my exams so that I did not have to endure such pathetic feelings even after getting good marks. It was on one of these days when my *Ammi* entered into the room and suggested, "Zaid dear, you could join your Abbu's business. He is growing old and might need your assistance and opinions."

I recoiled at the suggestion outright, but later contemplated over it and assented to *Ammi*'s suggestion eventually. Early morning the very next day, I got ready to leave with Abbu, since he always left the house at 9 AM without amiss. My breakfast tray was placed next to my father's on the table, and I regretted it as soon as I saw it because I was not habitual of having meals with him. I was propelled by my *Ammi* to the table regardless.

"You should try getting along with your Abbu now. After all, you will have to stand by him permanently through thick and thin," said she.

I approached the table slowly and calmly, consoling myself and trying to placate my shivering heart.

"Come on, Zaid! You could dare to dine with your lovely and respectable father," Abbu invited.

"Assalamualaikum, Abbu," I greeted him and pulled a chair next to him. He lifted his head to look at me, grimaced upon seeing my face and replied with a curt greeting. I aptly perceived his response that he was not even a bit convinced with the idea of me joining him in his business. Suddenly, I had the urge to irritate *Abbu* as much as I could, since I had plenty of free time now, and even the support of my *Ammi* to go with him. I munched on my sandwich and drowned my tea hastily before getting ready to leave.

"Ask him to go alone. I will come after 12 PM, as I have to get a haircut," said my father. Quite beautifully, he had snubbed my aspiration of driving to work in our car. I left home and boarded the bus somehow to reach Mundka–a backward area in South Delhi. Though I had only been there thrice before and its location was somewhat vague in my mind, I remembered the huge gate at the entrance. As I entered, I observed the place infested with dirty plastic bags everywhere. There were sacks upon sacks of polyester, L.D., P.P. & cable wires all around me. No waste management system was in place and I felt smothered by the dust and the sticky atmosphere. However, I held my ground and encouraged myself to remain strong. I coughed a few times to purge myself out of this discomfiture. When I opened my eyes, I found a man standing in front of me.

"Hello! I'm Rashid, your father's accountant," he introduced himself with pride.

"I am Mohd. Zaid! The son of your *babuji,*" I replied. He took me to the main site and asked me to sit.

"Could you please acquaint me with the files and the kinds of plastic here?" I asked Rashid, the accountant. He followed through with my instruction. Gradually, I began feeling quite assiduously responsible, but it dissolved as soon as *Abbu* arrived at the work place. I stood up from my chair upon seeing him. "*Abbu*, I am through with all the files and the goods..." I started.

"Who asked you to take charge and poke your nose into my mercantile dealings?" he interrupted, submerging my words and flagging my enthusiasm with such a raucous reward for my assertion. I took myself aside, gauging the situation as well as my father's nonsense.

After a while, he started from the beginning and proved that all the things I had learned all morning were meaningless. I became resolute not to speak anything regarding his business anymore because it was not mine. Once again, I was struck with the perennial question that always disconcerted me that why was it always I who got trampled by my own father's words at every occasion in my life? I was lost in such pathetic thoughts when I heard someone calling me casually.

"Ahh…something pathetic again," I babbled and returned to *Abbu*.

"Go to the nearby tea stall and get three cups of tea with *namkeen,*" he ordered. At the receiving end, I felt no better than a wretched orphan sent to do his petty jobs. Regardless, I was craving for some hot beverage too, and left to get tea as ordered. When I got back with the three cups and had no sooner placed the tray on the table, Rashid grabbed one. The next was taken by Daulat Ram – a friend of *Abbu,* and the last one I offered to my *Abbu,* remaining a non-entity myself. This time, I was filled with a contemptuous feeling. I left the shop at once and sat on a bench under a fragile looking tee. Birds were chirping above me. For a moment, I wanted to shoot them shut, but the next moment, their song started to assuage my sorrows. I took great delight in seeing them flit from one twig to the another.

In a way, they also had the job of making a perfect nest for themselves to have a blissful and secure abode, besides getting food for their young ones, and they worked autonomously. They had a mutual understanding between them which never existed between *Abbu* and I. I had accepted the fact that such harmonising chemistry that existed among all non- human creatures could never be in our life. Time whizzed past quickly and when I squinted at my watch the next time, it showed that I had devoted three full hours to my catharsis. I turned my head up to the Almighty and prayed to not get trampled upon by

Abbu again. I reached the mosque situated at a stone's throw from that place and performed the *Asar Namaz* (evening prayer). After having worshipped, I definitely felt like a feather. It was time to go back to my Abbu, though I had no inclination for it, to see if any work awaited my return.

No sooner had I reached, *Abbu* emerged before me, accompanied by Rizwan uncle. When his gaze fell upon me, he became severely furious and said, "What the hell are you doing here?"

I had no words for him and was about to get run over by his admonitions again when another uncle, Mohd. Irfan, suddenly brought up the topic of his mercantile affairs in Kashmir and gestured at me to slip away. I did not let the opportunity pass and vanished from their sight immediately. I was fortunate to have Mohd. Irfan as my eldest uncle who was caring and had a sense of obligation towards his family. He understood well how unfair *Abbu* usually was with me.

Abbu had five brothers and a pair of cunning parents, but he thought he was the most blessed man on earth to be continuing the legacy of his family. The reality was, however, that what he cherished and loved as family did not include his own wife or children, but his siblings and parents only. He had always maintained a contemptuous eye for *Ammi* and the four of us children.

I had understood early on that despite being the son of a businessman, I would have to confront many precarious situations and serious impediments in my life. All of my uncles were very heedful of their respective families and made their budgets spacious enough to meet all their demands on time. They never even hesitated to borrow for the sake of their respective families' happiness. I often asked *Ammi* why had we been allotted such a roguish father, but she always admonished me in return, "We should thank God for at least giving you a father who gave you his name."

I was sitting on the deck outside the godown, lost in my thoughts for I don't know how long, when I heard Rashid's voice, "Zaid, have you planned to stay here for good? It's 7 o'clock." I got up hastily, pulled out of my contemplation, and was taken aback when I realized that I had been sitting there for hours. I had started to feel very sluggish by that time, courtesy the open-armed welcome that I had received that day. I had neither had my lunch nor dinner, and knew that I wouldn't land a morsel before reaching home. I shook my head to clear my thoughts and returned to *Abbu* who was already growing eager to go home. We got into the car and departed for home, never exchanging a word with each other still.

"Dear, what was your first day like?" *Ammi* asked as I reached home. I was feeling so inactive and exhausted that I could not answer her. She intuited that it must not have been a very lucky day for me. "I want to dine…please, get me some food quickly," I requested her, feeling ravenous with hunger.

She had prepared some delicious fish for me, and my appetite grew even more upon seeing it. All my pains dissolved into thin air as I had my fill and drowned it with two glasses of chilled water. Soon after, I slumped onto my mattress and did not move at all. I already felt too sick of my father and sleep seemed to be the only means to recover myself from the insipid adventure I had had with him at Mundka.

Rashid's Deceit

I woke up very early the next day and felt enormous power to deflect the insulting onslaughts of *Abbu* because I had had a dream the night before that exhorted me to walk ahead and make my avenue to ascension with a stoic determination. I perceived my dream very sagaciously and knew that I could outwit *Abbu* by behaving rebelliously with him before other people, but I discarded this idea because I did not wish to disregard *Ammi*'s sacrifice in bringing me up. I jolted out of my bed and started getting ready for work, for I looked no better than a gorilla with my ruffled hair and a swollen demonic face, testimony to the serene sleep I had had.

I left with my father that day. "You had better kept yourself away from the accounts. There is Rashid to deal with them," *Abbu* ordered sternly. I held completely the opposite view, thinking that I had all the right and reason to know every aspect of our financial flow. This time, I decided not to head straight for it, but to wait for the right time to check those accounts which were kept in privacy from my eyes. An hour later, we reached the office and I was ordered to keep close tabs on the labourers, so I did. It went well for a few days, but I hadn't got a good enough opportunity yet to take a look at those business accounts.

After about a week, God favored my situation and *Abbu* fell sick. He instructed me to go to work all alone, and contrary to my intuition, handed me his car keys too. I felt overwhelmed with joy that I could drive the car all by myself, and at such length too. It was a great feeling indeed, and I decided to test the limits of my driving abilities instead of moving cautiously like an apprentice. My father drove excruciatingly slow, taking about two hours to cover up the distance from Delhi to Ghaziabad, and to travel with him was no better than sitting on a bed of nails. I got to the go-down in twenty minutes that day and surprised everyone. Rashid had reached there early and I found him at my father's chair, whispering something stealthily to his younger brother. They broke apart upon hearing the sound of my heavy strides. I suspected that they were conspiring about something ugly. Regardless, I calmed myself down and took my seat.

"Where is Farooq bhai?" he asked.

"He has a mild fever, so he could not come today," I replied. He informed me that a few samples were to be inspected that day, so I checked them and permitted him to get goods in that material as soon as possible. I wanted to gradually bring myself into the good books of my father, so I took every decision quite judiciously.

While everyone had taken to their tasks in the go-down, I turned to the Almirah that contained the accounts files. I was just about to open it when Gopal, another accountant, stepped in and cooed, "Junior sa'ab ji is tackling the business today." Gopal had been working there for *Abbu* for over a decade.

"Yes, actually *Abbu* is down with fever at home, so I had to come alone today," I replied politely, perhaps because I had a fair understanding with him. "I did not see you yesterday," I said to him.

"I was on leave due to some personal engagement," he replied while opening the almirah. I offered to lend him a hand in his work, which he accepted cordially. He drew out a stack of accounts and placed them on the table, while I started going through them one by one. My eyes grew wide and I was absolutely dumbstruck. The hidden mystery had been revealed. 'Shit! Shit! Shit!' I repeated in my head. We were in deficit of about a million rupees or so.

"I think we should each have a cup of tea," said Gopal and left the room, perhaps understanding that I needed a moment alone to absorb the latest revelation. I went through the accounts again and again until I understood the whole gamut. We were surviving a loss of 3.5 million rupees plus interest at that time. I felt quite done in and held my head in my hands.

"Dear, how did you find the accounts?" Gopal asked upon returning with two cups of tea.

"They exceed the limits of being terrible!" I said with discontentment. All of my strength was beaten down that day upon coming to know that we were trapped in such a vicious debt, without even having experienced the full swing of life. It was all undoubtedly because of *Abbu* who presided over this business. Despite our meagre situation, *Ammi* had never urged him to take loans. In fact, she always managed with the small amount of money that *Abbu* gave her. All four of us children studied in government schools, so we did not bother his pocket much. None of us was given the right to probe into his official matters, nor his personal life. We had been kept in a painful oblivion. I had to get to the bottom of this. For a moment, I suspected Gopal too and checked his accounts after he left, but to no benefit.

I passed my day rather painfully, and left early because I wanted to share the whole story with *Ammi*. I trusted her to find the best remedy to this situation.

Upon reaching home, I pulled her out of the kitchen, saying, "*Ammi*, I have something very shocking to tell you." Confused, she followed after me. "*Ammi*, I checked through all of Abbu's accounts, and do you know what I got?"

"Did you find something amiss, Zaid?" she asked, perplexed.

"We are steeped in a debt of around 3.5 million."

"What?" Her mouth was agape with surprise and she froze in her spot. I shook her to bring her back to her senses. "Oh! This is incredibly horrible," she murmured to herself as she did not want to express the grimness of her feelings. "Son, you can help your father repay the debt, but I wonder what the cause is behind this steep ruin."

"I can't think of a single reason, but all this has been happening for a decade with Abbu there," I told *Ammi*.

"What different has happened in this last decade?" *Ammi* thought aloud, reflecting upon a possible reason behind such a ruinous debt.

"What dreadful mistakes have you made today?" my Abbu rammed into the room just then without alerting us and sat on the bed.

"Nothing, Abbu Ji. I handled everything well," I replied submissively, feeling petrified by the whole situation.

"I don't believe it, but I'll deal with that tomorrow," he declared patronisingly and left.

The next day, we reached the godown together, perhaps for the last time. My eyes hunted for Gopal, as I wanted to make sure whether or not he had told *Abbu* anything about the previous day. Finally when I caught up with him, I found out that he had not spoken to my father for two days because he had lost his cell phone. Everything was going smoothly, but only till the evening.

"How dare you touch my accounts!? Who asked you to do so?" My father exploded. "Thank God for my loyal worker who told me about your audacity!" He shouted, his moustache twitching. I caught sight of Rashid standing not far behind, with a sly smile on his face. I got determined to settle scores with him sometime in the future.

As I had expected at the very beginning, I could not go on for more than a month at my father's workplace. "You had better stay at home from now on. No need to return to my godown." *Abbu* snapped in rage. I found no suitable words to pacify *Abbu*, and even if I had, I could never have used them to convince him because he was a cantankerous man who could never look past his prejudice against me. I passed the rest of the day roaming around. At around 2 PM when *Abbu* was out, I went to the washroom to pee and found Rashid there. He was whispering something to his younger brother, just like I had seen him the previous day. I did not let this golden opportunity slip by and dashed towards him. I caught him by his collar and pushed him into the washroom, "How dare you make interventions in our personal matters? What have you told *Abbu*?" I interrogated.

"Bhai, I don't understand what you are saying," he responded, feigning ignorance. I did not want to hear these words and was about to strangulate him, but when I found him breathing heavily, I had to leave him. He disappeared out of the stall at once. However, I concluded that he was a man of straw, a pernicious being who would cost us dearly.

The Brawl Over Debt

I reached home with *Abbu* at 10 PM that day.

"Let it be known to your son that he can never become a businessman like me, nor does he have any right to intervene into my accounts." *Abbu* exploded at the dining table. "They are accounts of my business," he stressed.

"What happened?" my *Ammi* asked rather meekly. "Your son has been peeping into my accounts in my

absence, without even seeking my permission first." He roared more angrily than before.

"So what if he has? He will inherit the same business one day."

I was taken by surprise at *Ammi*'s bold words. She was speaking so for the first time in twenty years of their marriage.

"What? It is my business. I have built it by virtue of my hard work. What right does he have to appraise my accounts? Besides, I have two competent accountants to handle my accounting operations, and they can provide me with a far more able assistance." He let out in one breath.

"Are they the same intellectual and able accountants who assisted you, their master, into entering into such an enormous debt?" asked my *Ammi,* taking charge of the conversation. "It's about 3 million, if I am not wrong." Her words held a magical strength and force as she assailed him with these bitter questions authoritatively, yet her tone revealed a conscious and considerate wife. I watched on like a mute child, not daring to poke my nose between these two reasons of my existence.

It seemed the advent of a revolution in my family, spearheaded by *Ammi*.

"Who are you to question me about the private matters of my business? You have nothing to do with it." Stormed *Abbu* as he flipped up the salad platter on the table in anger. The glass platter shattered to pieces on the table and a splinter slashed through *Ammi*'s arm. I rushed to her side when I saw her hand starting to bleed. "Hey, you! Coming to stop me? A little boy growing up on my charity!"

This abominable remark left me dumbfounded. My younger sisters and brother also got up upon hearing this tumultuous bout. I was in tears now, but *Abbu*–the callous and despotic man remained standing without any regret. My sisters rushed to my *Ammi*, and cleaned and dressed her wound with cotton and bandage. It was a night full of sorrow, but also a stimulant for us to stand up for our right of living.

My father had a peaceful sleep that night, but the rest of our lives just couldn't get back to normalcy. The next day, he woke up as if it was just another normal day for him. *Ammi* served him breakfast as usual, because she thought that it would be sacrilegious if she failed to carry out the basic duties of an Indian woman towards her husband. I did not have to accompany him today because of the whole tragedy of the previous two days.

"Zaid! It seems that you will have to build your dreams in finance by your own initiative." *Ammi* said upon noticing the disappointment on my face.

"But I have received enough from Abbu for expressing my assertion." I replied in a low voice.

"You don't understand me," she said. "My dear, you will have to choose a field apart from your Abbu's business," she continued. "You are mature and bold enough to deal with the prevailing situation and utilize your time well before you become eligible for graduation. You must pull up your socks and make the best of this year that you've got free."

"There is a call for you, bhaijaan," cried aloud my youngest sister. I went to attend the call.

"Hey Zaid! What's up, buddy?" It was Amir on the other side.

"Quite boring," I replied.

"I have a remedy to dilute your insipidity. It's the annual fest at Hansraj College tomorrow," he spoke jubilantly.

"What do we have to do with that?" I asked.

"We have been asked to broom and sweep the place clean," he taunted and burst out laughing. "My poor lamb, there will be fantastic dance performances for us to watch, along with a food fete to enjoy," he explained.

"Okay, what time is it?" I asked, having no desire to let go of this opportunity.

"At 2 PM. Meet me at *Gol Chakkar* without delay. The entire group will be there," he said and cut the line.

I reached the stated place exactly on time the next day.

"Long time, Zaid!" I heard Amir's voice from behind me. The rest of them arrived soon and all five of us boarded a bus to go to the fest, anticipating to have a blast there. When we reached the college campus, we figured that we had to have either the identity card or purchase a ticket to enter. Unfortunately, we all were destitute of either, but returning from a place like this without having fun was not in my blood. "We could leap over that wall easily," I suggested, and everyone agreed on it. It wasn't the first time that we were taking such a recourse, and were quite accustomed to it. Sameer, who had a bulky frame, had some trouble landing and crashed to the ground. However, God was in his favor that day since the ground below was soft and damp. He was sure to have broken his knees otherwise. "My bull! Are you all right?" asked Honey, another friend of ours.

Sameer stood up right away and dusted himself off, as if a minor fall could not put a dent on his enormous strength. We proceeded on to participate in the thrill of the fest. The premise was lined by fast-food stalls and my friends bought a glass of mocktail from one of them. We sipped on it one by one, since we couldn't afford two.

"Hey, handsome! Come here," a gorgeous girl hailed at me loudly.

"Zaid, she is calling out to you. You should go," Honey said and pushed me towards her.

I walked on with a cool gait, pretending to be a genuine student, even though I was neither a scholar nor a college-goer.

"You seem to be an innocent boy among the laggards there," she said bluntly. I noticed that she had a good stature, bob cut hair, and astoundingly sharp features.

"Yes, I have come from the age of Adam," I replied, mimicking her lofty tone. Her lips sealed up for a minute, replacing the broad smile that had danced on them just a moment ago.

"Pah! What an old guy to be standing amongst us. Can you even dare to compete with us academically to gain admission into our college?"

I knew she was trying to take me in with her big words and deviously rhetorical English that didn't make complete sense to me at that time. I stood no chance to survive the war of eloquence which did not seem to be ending soon. I left the place wordlessly, the laughter of those girls ringing in my ears.

"Who was that bitch, Zaid?" Amir asked inquisitively, wanting to know word-for-word what conversation had taken place between us. I did not even know her name. "She was an inspiration to chase after the eloquent generation in the guise of a wicked girl," I said and narrated to him all that she had said, regardless of whether he understood my words or not. My guess is, he didn't.

It was the turning point in my life, when I became determined to achieve something. I went to the library later that same day and made up my mind to meet that girl again and outwit her before a mass of people, as she had done today. I was dead set on working hard for it. I borrowed multiple books of English from the library that could aid me in my ambition. I was now bent on learning English so immaculately that nobody would be able to shame me in this specific realm.

My goal for the year was set, and I felt very calm since it was all in my hands now. I had been left alone to follow my will by *Abbu*, and didn't have the commitment to attend any classes that year either. Day in and day out, I toiled harder. I visited the popular tourist places where I met with foreigners to assimilate aptly to their accent, although my own accent had been innately clean. I was thankful to God that my diction was not made impure by my local dialect. Days passed on quickly, while my practice of English got better day by day. I gave it six hours without exception everyday, cramming piles upon piles of books. After about a month, I felt that I had acquired some competence in English speaking and debate.

It was 26th January, Republic day, and I needed some pocket money for partying with my friends. I implored *Ammi* for it and she spoke to *Abbu*.

"I don't remember registering a hundred rupees of pocket money to him every month for such tiny occasions," he countered harshly.

I was now reduced to a mere worker in the house, who was to be assessed for the service he performed in a month. I fell into a reflective trance once again, as *Abbu* often made me, but my *Ammi* consoled me like an angel and gave me some money from her own purse. I went to see my friends that day with a burden in my heart.

I thought of engaging myself in a job of sorts to gain some financially autonomy, since I was done facing the humiliation always inflicted upon me by *Abbu*. I was on the street, rambling to myself about all this near the mosque when I heard someone talking about God very passionately. I couldn't see who it was since there was traffic hiding the speaker and the listener from me. I rushed towards them with a curiosity to know what was happening. It was one of the *Jamaat*'s Heads, clad in a long white cloak, trying to make people understand the religious tenets and principles. I approached the man and greeted him in the Islamic manner. His eyes sparkled upon seeing me. I introduced myself in English then.

"We are from Saudi Arabia. Who are you, my dear son?" he asked as he embraced me warmly. I understood then what the matter was about. Their native language was Arabic, which none in our locality could understand, so they were using English to make communication and relay the essence of their thoughts, but the poor inhabitants of our neighbourhood would not understand English either.

"May I help as a translator?" I offered gladly.

"Of course, my son. We will be thankful to you. God will bestow numerous blessing upon you for such kindness," he said, looking very pleased with me. I kept translating his words in my fractured understanding of English for an hour. Some of my uncles were present there too, and took my translating abilities as a precious talent. When the discussion came to an end, I took my leave and walked away with a renewed sense of confidence. I began to feel that all my hard work was finally paying off. During these six months, I had almost detached myself from all my former friends because not one productive deed made a part of their daily activities, while education was a matter of joke to them. I had replaced them with books as my new best buddies.

"Zaid, how are you, my child?" I heard someone calling after me that day. It was Hamid uncle, my father's acquaintance. I greeted him back respectfully.

"I saw your caliber in speaking English today. How did you learn it?" He asked interestedly.

"Uncle, all that you saw is the result of hours spent on studying the language heuristically." I replied to him honestly.

"Would you like to teach my son, Ali? He is in 11th class and is becoming a nag for me day by day," he offered. "I want to have him engaged in a rewarding course, and English speaking is the best choice."

I remained tongue-tied for a moment, but brought myself back to my senses and replied, "Hmm... certainly, uncle. You can send Ali whenever he is free. I will take care of it." I had completely forgotten that it was up to the teacher to pick up a time to teach his students.

"Okay, he shall be at your house tomorrow at 6 PM."

I rushed back home, leaping with joy that I had finally found a means to bear my own expenses. My (self) education was finally proving worth a career. Soon after Ali, I got five more students to teach and I became financially independent. My new profession gave me a new persona, a new confidence and groomed my personality to gain a better reputation. I started teaching even those students who were older than me. Initially, it shocked me when they addressed me as 'sir', specially the older ones, but I soon got used to it and felt that I deserved the grand salutation.

English Classes

A year had passed since I started my classes on spoken English, and they were progressing by leaps and bounds. I had now shifted the venue of my classes to our old paternal house which had been lying unoccupied for the past few years. Although it was in a secluded location, I found it to be in my favour because I could teach my students there in perfect serenity and quietude. I worked dedicatedly to upgrade my institute and gathered much admiration in the neighbourhood, though I had not expected such a huge success out of it.

Since my free year was now over, I was required to get admission into some college for graduation and take the golden opportunity that I had been awaiting so eagerly. I opted for a B.Com course by correspondence, since it offered me ample time to continue my latest profession, while also pursuing interests like acting, football and guitar.

One sunny Sunday, I found myself feeling somewhat agitated with my surroundings, and my head felt very heavy too. It had happened suddenly, for I had gone to bed the day before with a healthy mood.

"Zaid, will you have parantha or bread for breakfast?" my *Ammi* asked, as was usual on Sundays. I did not reply to her, and buried my head under the pillow. When I heard her ask again, I simply shouted back, "Only a cup of tea."

There was dead silence on the other side. I found myself feeling guilty for being so harsh with my loving *Ammi*. My ego had been fed quite so by this time that it resisted me from apologizing to my *Ammi*. I left my house soon after and spent the next five hours at my institute, suffocating from inside. This went on for about a week, and I scarcely spoke to my *Ammi* or siblings. I restricted my presence to either my room or my institute. I got irritated for no reason. I didn't have a clue of what had gone wrong with my mood. I simply could not relate to anything around me. All my family members seemed roguish and backward. It was absolutely ridiculous, since I had never physically been separated from them for long.

The thought kept tormenting me for days. I had a fierce desire to run away. It was an unnatural force that had overpowered me and motivated me to abandon everything.

Back home, I went to sit next to the window in my room and looked outside, completely sunk in my thoughts. My heart felt like it was being gagged by an evil spirit that had taken hold of me entirely.

"How are you feeling, Zaid?" my *Ammi* once asked dearly, and the dam of my emotions broke. I clang to her and burst into tears. The next day, my *Ammi* was to see a doctor for some consultation.

"Where is *Ammi*?" I asked Shazia, my youngest sister.

"She is out for some important work," she replied. "Am I not important enough? Do I not hold any worth in the family? Are you all just fed up with me?"

I regurgitated foolishly. It was all coming out of my capricious mind.

"It's not like that, she did not even inform us. She left in a rush," she explained.

"You all are stupid and just a nuisance." I exclaimed, then began scratching my head, wondering what had gotten into me since the last few days. What had changed me so overnight?

"What spell are you under?" *Ammi* asked pleading, when she returned.

"I don't hold any value in this family. There is nothing here for me. I am as good as a step-child to you." I simmered with rage.

"This is only your flawed perception. We all care for you, and you certainly are my real son. Please do not repeat these heartbreaking words ever," she warned me.

My father arrived just then and we all had to disperse as usual. Such was the situation with my family that we could never share a light-hearted moment together. My father's presence was like a hurricane which swept everyone away.

"What the hell are you cooking today?" he fired his question towards *Ammi*.

"It's fish. I thought you would like it, since it's your favorite dish. Also, it helps control diabetes," she elaborated.

"Okay, that's good. Bring it quickly," he ordered impatiently.

"Here it is! If you need anything else, please call out to me. I will cook some rice too," she said and walked back to the kitchen.

My mother's love for us persisted despite my father's cruel behavior. He switched on the T.V. and started relishing the fried fish. The very next moment, his phone rang.

"Oh, God! These rascals! I cannot have a peaceful moment. They won't even let me have my food. I am sure to die sooner than later," he rambled furiously like a rogue. "Hello," he spoke into the phone. "I have just gotten home, and will ring you back in a while," he answered gently. I noted how all his anger had died down mysteriously towards the end of the call. There was something fishy at the bottom for sure.

"Hajira!" he called out to *Ammi*. "Take this crap of a fish away from me. You don't have any sense of cooking. You just spoil whatever I bring home."

All the love and labor *Ammi* had put into making diner was laid waste in just a moment.

"What happened? I'll fry it again, just give me a minute," she beseeched him like a maid under sheer atrocity.

"No need. This is hell! I will have dinner at Rizwan's house tonight. You can neither cook nor lead a family. You all depend on my earnings," he roared loudly. "Look at your defunct son! He's so careless and keeps looking out the window as if his mother was dancing on the street," he reprimanded me indirectly. I was in another room, yet he was loud enough to be audible.

After having done the damage, he left murmuring. It was quite apparent that he had deliberately shunned the meal. I had full trust in my *Ammi*'s culinary skills. She had been cooking in this house for twenty years and never had the food cooked by her tasted bad. It was unreasonably strange. I could not understand whether it was the force of Almighty or something else that was ruining all of us so severely. We had failed to find a reason behind it.

I gathered all my siblings and *Ammi* in a room to deliberate over this ongoing trauma, yet it proved futile! We burst into tears rather than producing any consolatory words for each other. Perhaps, we were too young to understand and survive all of it. Abbu headed for the loo. The toilet was right at the entrance of our house. We were sitting in the middle room and could hear his footsteps clearly. Shazia tried to divert us by talking about her progress at school, for she had gotten immensely perturbed by all this. Saif shut her up then and there, and she could not proceed any further.

As a result, we returned to the perpetual barbarity of our lives. Abbu now rushed back to our room and smacked the door with full force. He was unstoppable! "Open the door if you dare!" he shouted monstrously. Furthermore, we received a flurry of obnoxious abuses, mostly directed towards *Ammi*. I stepped forward to unlock the bolt and answer back, but *Ammi* held me back. We kept hearing his words as he ranted and raved thunderously, but did not open. We knew that he would soon leave for Rizwan uncle's house for dinner, and that's exactly what he did. There was a pin drop silence outside the door after a while. We kept absolutely mum for about fifteen more minutes. It felt as if the entire universe had stalled and turned deaf and mute.

I had never dreamt that things would come to this. Abbu had clearly expressed that it was agonising for him to be with us anymore, especially because of his growing hatred towards *Ammi*. We had no choice but to remain patient. Given the situation, I was successively growing pessimistic about my existence. At the tender age of seventeen years and four months, I had no idea how to deal with all this without breaking down emotionally. Despite having shouldered most of the household responsibilities by my part-time teaching, there was no appreciation, motivation or congratulations for me. It was all awful.

In Abbu's absence, we kept discussing the situation all night. We had a feeling that he would not return that night. We were quite sure of it because of a couple of reasons. One, Abbu shared each and every matter of his personal life with his brothers and parents, regardless of the gravity or privacy of the matter. Two, he loved to sit by his sisters-in-law and give them matter for gossip, and he craved for such moments.

One thing was certainly obvious that he would have a grand time with Rizwan uncle and the family in his house. He would have his desired meal cooked by Shama aunty, Rizwan uncle's wife. It was a painful predicament to accept and *Ammi* deserved a trophy for having adapted to such an atmosphere. We finally concluded our discussion, since my siblings had school the next day, and went to sleep. We closed the doors and tried to sleep, though none of us could get any. I turned my sides incessantly, as did the others, unable to rid my mind of the whole drama stirring inside.

Rashid's Family

"Wake up, Zaid! Don't you have to get ready to go to Mundka with your Abbu?" *Ammi* asked, shaking me awake.

I thought it to be a nightmare, but it was in vain. "Umm... shall I go with him? He's turned insane, don't you realize it?" I mumbled. The plight of our family had been mounting and I wanted to break through my father's patriarchal dominance.

"Would you shut up now, Zaid!" *Ammi* gave me a tight slap across my face. It was one of those rare occasions when she seriously got furious. She knew what lessons to teach her kids and when. "He is your father, and you must hold utmost reverence for him. He is my husband and he runs this house," she further added.

"But *Ammi*..." I stopped. I could not say a word further at this point.

"In the light of Islam, parents are the most vital figures in one's life, and they ought to be obeyed under all circumstances and situations," she enlightened me. I spotted tears in her divine eyes which had been resting there permanently for quite some time. Their sudden emergence again pierced me poignantly. I did not wish to join Abbu's business any longer due to the innumerable bitter interactions in the past. Also, the disagreements between us had mounted up so speedily and fiercely in the past six months. Had it all happened because I had begun to own some household responsibilities? Had it taken such a shape due to my *Ammi*? I had no clue of what was coming my way.

"*Ammi,* I don't think I can be his helping hand anymore. He has already piled up a mammoth debt for us to live under. Furthermore, he does not trust me at all. Gopal and Rashid are more competent than I am as far as accounting, book keeping and his business marketing is concerned," said I, avoiding making eye contact with her.

"No, he is good at heart. Moreover, you can impress him with your skills. Try to comfort him and be his support. With the course of time, you will eventually become the boss. After all, every father works for his sons, and you're the eldest son. Make the most of this opportunity," she said in a single breath, and quite convincingly too. I had planned to escape by leaning on my coaching and graduation studies. "You can teach your students after a year or so too. Establishing his business should be more important than anything else for you right now. Once you get successful, I shall be the happiest." I didn't like her throwing water on the clay walls of my ambitions. "How about your graduation? Have you collected the study material from the university yet?" she asked curiously.

"Oh yes, my B.Com classes are commencing this month and I will need to visit the correspondence office for my books, since they haven't reached me yet," I answered confidently. She looked upset with my evasiveness and wanted me to be truthful at that moment.

"Zaid, you know what? I was over the moon when I gave birth to you on 11th August, at 5.15 AM on a

Monday because you were loved by the entire family. Let me also tell you that I faced the greatest amount of medical complications during your delivery, which did not happen with any of the other kids. I always cherish incredible success, therefore you can never bamboozle me," said *Ammi*. It struck me as an eye-opener, and I could not think of an appropriate response to what *Ammi* had just said.

"What should I do?" I asked her, scratching my head. She began to make tea for Abbu and me. I was still feeling unsure of what I should do. It was the month of June and we all hated going out in the scorching heat of Delhi. Mundka had become a horrible show for me by then, but I could not make *Ammi* upset at any cost. She was busy cooking breakfast, while simultaneously keeping an eye on me. She gauged my mood regarding how badly Mundka had tortured me. I got into the washroom which was right by the entrance of our house. It was my favourite place in. the house as I could be alone and solve all the complexities of my life sitting there in peace. I could spend as long as 35 minutes in the toilet at a time to relax. I feared that if Abbu came to know about my reluctance, it would be a fiery ordeal for me. We all lived under his terror.

"How long is it going to take for breakfast? It is 9.45 AM already and I am supposed to reach office early today," Abbu thundered in his stentorian voice.

"Yes, just two minutes," *Ammi* replied. She always tried to appease him, otherwise he would go on and on. It was the greatest sacrifice that she made for us everyday, and for the sake of their relationship.

Abbu's cell phone rang with the popular Nokia ringtone in vogue at that time. "Namaskar, Gopal! How many trucks are departing from Hyderabad? Has Yusuf bhai consigned the goods yet?" Abu asked Gopal and hung up in less than a minute. While he was busy

on the phone, I came out stealthily so that he would not learn of my lingering presence in the toilet.

"Zaid is going along with you today," *Ammi* told *Abbu*. I felt absolutely petrified, for *Abbu's* behaviour was always unpredictable! He alone could spoil even the most amazing occasions. "Please take him along so he learns the tricks of trade from you," *Ammi* requested. A shock wave ran down my body. I did not want to resume going to work with *Abbu*.

"How do you ensure that he would excel in the plastic waste industry? Do you guarantee that he would not poke his nose into my business accounts?" asked Abbu sternly. I prayed to God to help me evade this situation, but all was in vain!

"Yes, yes, he will do as you instruct," *Ammi* responded affirmatively. It seemed as if she had forgotten all about the debt that Abbu had earned over our heads.

"Both are the same," I said to myself.

"Zaid, get ready immediately. You are going to work with Abbu," *Ammi* ordered. I rushed to take shower, carrying a towel into the bathroom. It was obvious that nothing was happening in my favor. Turning on the tap, I thought of locking myself in for as long as it would take them to drop the idea of getting me involved in Abbu's business again. It was a pathetic idea! I even imagined drowning myself in a 1000 litre water reservoir in the house.

"Zaid, Abbu is waiting for you in the street," *Ammi* informed me, knocking at the door. It was an order for me to get out as soon as possible. I dropped those terrible ideas and sped up getting ready. On coming out, I quickly put on a white t-shirt and jeans. I skipped breakfast, thinking that Abbu would get even more angry if he got late.

"Zaid, have tea at least," *Ammi* offered, but I ignored everything in the interest of time.

A young boy walked into the house just then, calling out, "Zaid bhai, Zaid bhai."

"Yeah, what happened?"

"Your Abbu is waiting in his car for you," said he.

I picked up pace to get to the car, where I found him waiting in a grey safari suit. It was all happening out of my interest. He looked at me, then turned to get into his white Santro to drive. Near our residence, there was a red light where we had to halt.

"This is ridiculous!" pronounced Abbu. He desired a perfect world which probably had no vehicles on the road while he drove. I wanted to let him know that such a world was not possible, and one could not rule over the planet. "This is what makes life hell! You should have gotten ready a little early," he added further. To my surprise, his tone was calm and composed this time.

"I got late because of breakfast. I am sorry, it will never happen again," I apologized, lying through my teeth. We sped on when the light went green and reached the go-down within forty minutes. Abbu parked the car at the gate and we proceeded to 'Farooq Plastic' where my second innings were to start.

All the labourers greeted Abbu with 'Namaste, babuji!', but there were no greetings for me. On the contrary, people were startled with my presence and whispered among themselves as if I was going to sack them all. Their smiling faces turned profusely pale.

"Rashid, put this lunch box in the office," Abbu ordered. I felt glad that I hadn't been ordered to do it. Things felt a little different this time.

"Zaid, you may sit inside the office. I have some customers to deal with," said Abbu. A big smile grew on my face. This was happening for the first time.

"Thank you, Allah!" I said to myself.

That day went quite well, as Abbu treated me nicely and like a father for the first time. It was extremely rare for me to experience that. At 9 PM, we drove back home. On the way, he asked me, "Did you understand how customers are treated in this market? How to make more money? More importantly, you need to pay attention to the business ethics here."

"Hmm...sure, I will. It will take some time for everything to be in place and for me to settle in," I promised. He seemed impressed by my keenness.

Ammi opened the door with a big smile on her face. "Asslamualaikum *Ammi*!" I greeted her.

"Walaikumasslam, how was your day?" she enquired.

"Yeah, it was fine," I replied. *Ammi* looked quite happy, as if her dream had come true. I freshened up hurriedly and performed *wuzu* (ablution) religiously and without delay to offer all my missed prayers. "Allah, please maintain this niceness in Abbu forever!" I prayed.

"*Ammi*, how did you bring about this change in Abbu? He was so cheerful today and even advised me to improve my business skills," I shared with *Ammi*.

"Well, I made him understand that your son has grown up and he is more literate than Rashid and Gopal. Also, blood is thicker than water," *Ammi* said and smiled.

"Oh, I see! He was so nice to me today. I did not even have to bring tea from the tea vendors," I said, feeling happy and radiant. "But the labourers and the accountants are not happy with my return. What could be the reason for that?" I asked her.

"Zaid, it will take sometime. You are still new to them!" *Ammi* pacified me and told me to have an apple from the fridge. Abbu walked in just then, after having spent some time at Rizwan uncle's shop near our house. He smiled at *Ammi* and me. Smiled! It was absolutely unbelievable, unthinkable and unimaginable.

"Hajira, it's too hot today! Please get me some chilled water. It's tough to earn money these days," Abbu said and lit a cigarette.

"It is blistering hot. May Allah have mercy upon us! Would you like to have some mango shake or lemonade?" *Ammi* offered. I was glad to see *Ammi* smiling after so many days. All of us slept well that night.

The next day, Abbu and I went back to Mundka and I tried to take more control of the official nitty-gritties. All my unwanted feelings began to change due to my *Ammi*'s words–that things will take some time. Rashid was still a little uncomfortable with my presence, but Gopal was good. I initially lived with a mindset that people of the same faith gelled well sooner, but it was proven untrue. Gopal minded his own business and never indulged in trivialities, while

Rashid was frivolous, rebellious and an innate liar. This was perhaps because of their age difference, or where they had come from. Gopal hailed from Alwar, Rajasthan, while Rashid was from Badayun, Uttar Pradesh. The former had a jet-black complexion, while the latter was fair and handsome.

We all rested in the office for a while. It was a lean time for the entire market, and all the traders usually indulged in a quick nap after lunch. Gopal was dealing with a buyer outside and we could hear his voice, "LD is for Rs. 55 per kg, and grinding is Rs. 104."

Abbu, Rashid and I were inside the chamber. "Rashid, keep a close eye on Gopal," said Abbu to Rashid.

"Okay, babu ji. Don't worry!" assured Rashid.

It was quite strange for me to hear. Abbu looked at me, as if expecting me to contribute to the conversation, but I stayed quiet. At first, I failed to understand why Gopal was being discriminated against. Was it his faith or something else? Only God knew. I was curious to get to get to the bottom of it, but wondered who could enlighten me on it.

The sun was setting gradually, and I saw some buyers hopping in late in the evening.

"Babuji, it is great to see your son here. It was high time for him to come help you," one of them said and they all laughed jovially.

"Yes, you are right. He's seventeen now, and it is important for him to take on responsibilities as I did twenty-eight years ago," said Abbu.

One thing was clear that expectations had risen from all quarters. Also, I had decided not to look into Abbu's debtors' and creditors' account, as he disliked it. I weighed trucks on the weighing scale and prepared vouchers accordingly. I had nothing to do with cash. We drove back that night and got home at 9.45 PM.

After the greetings, *Ammi* asked me the usual question, "How was your day?"

I said, "Very good." Her smile was even wider than before.

"*Ammi*, why does Abbu not trust Gopal?" I asked. "What happened?" she looked curious and restless. "Well, nothing major. Abbu ordered Rashid to keep a close eye on him today. I don't understand it," I answered.

Ammi was in a fix and did not have an answer to it. "Let it be. Perhaps he is not working efficiently these days," *Ammi* replied, but I was not convinced. Moreover, she was the right person to solve this mystery.

A week passed by and it became a daily routine for me to go to Mundka, come rain or shine. I read the holy Quran everyday without fail. One day, *Ammi* asked me to read the holy book with its translation. The book is written in Arabic, which I somewhat knew how to read, write and speak, courtesy my preliminary *madarsa* education. She insisted that I read and understand all the tidings mentioned in it.

"Quran has the complete solution to the sufferings of mankind, and it leads us on the right path," *Ammi* told me. The right path and guidance was what I was desperately looking for.

"Okay, *Ammi*," I promised her I would do as she taught. She was the only person I was blindly obedient to on earth, so I went to Jama Masjid and got a bilingual copy of Quran (Urdu-Arabic). I carried it to Mundka everyday and would read through it with great interest and punctuality during breaks. This was something that Abbu liked immensely. By and by, people got familiar with me and the entire market came to know who I was. The only thing that I felt humiliated by was my Reliance CDMA budget cell phone that I had bought for a meagre fifteen hundred rupees by saving up on the tuition money from my students. Its screen had innumerable scratches and it looked ugly.

Within two months, the labourers got accustomed to having me around. I brought in a fresh and dynamic perspective. The business was typically carried out in Hindi and manually, but I introduced 'English Vouchers' for the first time. It came as a good change. Both the accountants had initially looked uninterested in these vouchers, since they both knew nothing except Hindi. But I convinced them that English vouchers had been in the market for about two years already, and were late in getting on the bandwagon.

A well-known money lender, Rajesh Badgujjar visited us one evening. On seeing him, Abbu stepped forward to welcome him, as if two heads of rival clans were meeting for the first time.

"Gopal, get two cold drinks! Make sure they are extra chilled," Abbu ordered proudly and lit a cigarette for Rajesh. They both sat down in the open area of the go-down, while I was sitting inside the chamber, discussing some plastic products with Rashid. When Rajesh saw me, we exchanged a smile.

"Babu ji, is that your son? He looks like it," he said, pointing at me.

"Oh yes, he is. I bring him along so he may learn some skills of running a business," Abbu replied.

"That is nice! Has he completed his studies yet?" Rajesh asked. I anticipated Abbu to call me now, since he knew little of my academic progress, and so it happened.

"Zaid, come here!" he called out.

"Are you in 13th standard or 14th?" *Abbu* asked. I cringed at his words, but I had started to be more tolerant towards Abbu, more polite and respectful. It had all been because of the translated version of the holy Quran that I had started studying. The book had transformed me magically, making the duties towards my parents my utmost priority in life. Therefore, I shook off all the rebellious thoughts that I had against him. He was *Abbu*, my key to receiving all accolades in this temporal world and in the afterlife as well. So, I did not react to that awkward question.

"I am pursuing a degree in B.Com from DU," I replied.

"Oh! That's great. Well done!" complimented Rajesh. "Babu ji, don't force him to be here because he can do better in his studies. As far as I know, nobody has even passed class 10th in your entire clan," he taunted.

"Rajesh, he has to manage it all for the sake of this business, to create his own identity. There's no omelet without breaking the eggs," Abbu defended. Rajesh had touched my soul with his statement. *Ammi*'s teachings had great influence over me at the same time. Through Quran, she wanted to instil righteous behavior towards my parents in me, specially towards Abbu. I had begun to consider Abbu as my torchlight, his verdict was at the apex of all.

"Babu ji, get him a better phone at least," he said, gesturing towards the phone in my hands. "It does not suit your stature," he added salt further. Abbu had to think really hard now. All this talk was getting on his nerves.

"He can get as good a phone as he wants when he establishes himself. He needs to prove himself first. You see, I built up my life and made all my major purchases myself, and I expect the same out of him," he replied. Having heard that, I excused myself and got occupied in preparing the vouchers. Rajesh might have been right in saying that I needed a fairer treatment, but I was simply abiding by the Quran, and I paid no further attention to that incident. I picked up pace in building a good rapport with the buyers and the labourers. We got back home at 9.30 PM as usual that night. I had grown fairly comfortable with my routine now.

On the coming Friday, we went to Rajdhani park which was about 1.5 kilometers from our office to offer the *Juma Namaz* (Friday prayers). Abbu, Rashid and I reached there in our car. The prayer began at 1.30 PM and was completed by 1.50 PM. This prayer is mandatorily offered in a congregation. Hence, the *masjid* (mosque) was jam-packed. I stepped out of the mosque and saw Rashid waiting for Abbu and me down the street.

"Has Abbu not come out yet?" I asked Rashid.

"Zaid bhai, he's gone to my house to meet my abba and Amma," he revealed.

"Oh! Where do you live?" I asked curiously.

"The third house in this lane is ours, we have a rented house. Bhai, do you see the one where those kids are playing?" He pointed out the exact location. I couldn't guess what business Abbu might have there, but remained quiet. Abbu came out after a while and we traveled back to the go-down.

"Zaid, I would like to tell you something. Rashid lives near that masjid and I had gone there to meet his Amma. They're extremely poor. That is why I went to give them some money. They have nine kids – five sons and four daughters," Abbu said proactively. "Rashid has a sister too who got divorced just a month ago, and she's just 22. Poor lass!" he added.

"Oh! May God set things right for them," I wished, however I felt something fishy about the whole ordeal because *Ammi* had never discussed it with me. And Abbu had told me all before I had even raised a question. Abbu never explained himself to me.

On reaching home, I asked *Ammi* straightaway, "Do you know that Rashid's family lives in Delhi? And that his sister has been divorced recently?"

"Yes, I do. They are living in a terrible hand to mouth situation. May Allah bless them," replied *Ammi*.

"Also, why does Abbu visit his family? He even supports them financially," I revealed in a fit of rage.

"Financially?" She was surprised now. She had only started to demand a clarification, when Abbu knocked at the main door and cleaned his throat. We had to terminate the conversation right there.

At about 1 AM when Abbu had slept, I said to *Ammi*, "He should not support them at all. I know Rashid very well, he keeps chewing on the beetle leaf all day long. If he's so poor, he must cut down on his expenses. It's as simple as that." *Ammi* tried to dismiss the topic, but I was not to be placated.

"He gives me Rs. 4200/- every month to run the house," *Ammi* revealed for the first time.

"What? Is that all? This is peanuts!" I exclaimed, but soon realized that I couldn't speak that way about him.

"So what? You are fine, hale and hearty! Aren't you?" She was still glad, grateful and content, punctually thanking the Almighty five times a day for all that she had been granted.

"Well, he may be supporting them with a little unsubstantial amount," *Ammi* said, defending Abbu.

"Whatever it is, it is wrong!" I vented.

"You're not entitled to measure the rightfulness of it. Let him do as he deems fit. He fulfils all our needs," said *Ammi*. I felt embarrassed and crestfallen at her words, and hit the sack for the night.

Abbu Falls Sick Again

The city welcomed monsoon three months later. It was raining cats and dogs in Delhi, and everybody remained at home. I thought of chilling out once the rain would stop, as the weather was absolutely pleasant, but plans often get spoilt in the eleventh hour.

"Zaid, go to the go-down once the rain ceases, I need to get a hair-cut," said Abbu. I turned to *Ammi* and grimaced, as if she was responsible for the rain and his hair cut. No sooner did it stop raining, Abbu stepped out to get his haircut. It was about 12 PM and I was in no mood to deal with buyers and labourers. Moreover, the roads were all nasty and water-logged. A boy of seventeen years has a right to have a nice time with friends on such days, regardless. When I said all this to *Ammi,* she consoled me by saying, "Yes, you can go in the afternoon and come back early."

"No, I don't want to. A pleasant day like this has come after so many months. Please *Ammi,* please," I requested.

"Don't you want to support your father? Is that what you are saying? If you don't take control of our business, you will end up being an employee at some mobile repair shop or a garment showroom in Karol Bagh," *Ammi* taunted me. I broke into a sweat when I pictured myself washing cars or selling ladies' garments or goggles in the marketplace.

"*Ammi,* please let me stay home for just one day," I requested, but she got irritated. Rarely had I seen her so upset or annoyed.

"Why don't you understand that you are his successor. If you sail through well, the business is all yours!" *Ammi* encouraged me.

"Okay, it is a curse to be the eldest son! I will go after lunch," I capitulated angrily. It started to rain torrentially just before lunch, around 1 PM. I got extraordinarily happy, for the plan to go to the go- down seemed to have capsized. However, it was only momentary, and the rain stopped after twenty minutes. *Ammi* kept staring at me till I finally left for Mundka by bus.

Most of the labourers were on leave that day too due to the water-logging, though both the accountants were present. Despite that, I enjoyed full ownership of the office for the first time and took my place on Abbu's chair. It was an emotional and inspirational moment for me.

"Rashid, get me a Coke and some Good-day biscuits," I ordered. The backward region of Mundka didn't have much to offer for snacks, so I remained content with biscuits, which was a big deal for most traders.

"Here is your Coke. The biscuits were not available, and Saini's shop is closed today," Rashid said as he handed me the bottle. We sold only two sacks of P.P. throughout the day. I pocketed the Rs.1700 earned and headed home at nine as usual.

I found the main door to my house ajar as I entered. "*Ammi*...where are you?" I howled, but no response came from her. I panicked.

"Zaid," she finally responded from the drawing room.

"I've been looking for you," I said. I was in a jolly mood, but she did not ask how my day had been. In fact, she looked visibly distressed. "Is everything all right?" I asked.

"Your Abbu has fallen sick. He is down with typhoid fever," she replied hopelessly.

"He was fine in the afternoon when he went for a haircut?" I insisted.

"He was, but he got drenched in the rain on his way back. Then he slept with the AC on and got a mild headache. I gave him a Crocin for it."

"Then?" I enquired.

"We called in Dr. Manghani and he told us that it is typhoid," *Ammi* replied.

I was perturbed by this news. Abbu was deep in sleep, so I did not bother him. Instead, I rang up Dr.

A.K. Manghani to know more.

"There's nothing to worry about," he said. "Typhoid doesn't last for more than seven to ten days. It is a common communicable diseases here, and is caused by the bacterium Salmonella typhi. It spreads through contaminated water, or unhygienic food and drinks. I have prescribed some antibiotics for him, so please take good care of him. He will be all right."

Ammi handed me the doctor's prescription. It was all incomprehensible to me, so I rushed to the local pharmacist with it. There were many there who had come for typhoid medicines, I realized while standing in the queue. Everybody was in a hurry.

"Can I get these medicines, please?" I asked the compounder, handing him the prescription.

"Sure…here they are. Rs. 400 please," he demanded, keeping the medicines on the counter. I had the 1700 rupees from the go-down still with me, so I paid the amount from it.

Everybody at home was offering their evening prayers, and I joined them. It was unusual for me because I had never seen him get seriously ill, except mild stomachaches, headaches, or cough and cold. It rained throughout the night, while we got drenched in unease and anxiety. I had never felt so compassionate for Abbu before. Perhaps it was because *Ammi* had instilled in me the habit of reading the holy Quran. I learnt of the duties and gratitude towards parents in the light of God's words. As a result, I had been altered completely. I had realized that my hostile attitude towards Abbu was wrong. Those who have parents are certainly blessed. If Abbu was rigid, *Ammi* was my shield and it was enough that I had someone to call 'Abbu' at all. I said all this to myself in solitude. I could not speak to him, but I wished to touch his forehead and feet for the first time.

Before going to sleep, *Ammi* informed me that *Abbu* would not be able to make it to work the next day. Hence, I was supposed to assume leadership again. To my surprise, I felt hesitant to shoulder the responsibility. Abbu had a reputation for his rich experience and goodwill in the market, and I had gigantic shoes to fill in after him. I couldn't sleep thinking about all this. We tend to make stupid commitments to ourselves when we are down, just as I promised myself, 'I will set a new example in the market, both the accountants shall be at my mercy. Abbu & *Ammi* will feel so proud of me and my performance.'

The next day, I got to work alone and ensured that everything was in good shape. I instructed everyone to work efficiently, or they would be sacked. The accountants were shocked to know of Abbu's health. I knew it was all pretentious, for they were definitely craving for liberty and a pressure-free work environment in my Abbu's absence. Rashid was genuinely shocked for a moment, however, though it irked me for some reason. Things moved in right direction as I had imbibed the required skills from *Abbu* fairly well. I pulled out the list of all the creditors who had been on the ledgers for ages and made the accountants call them up and demand payment. Rashid followed up on the local creditors, while Gopal dealt with the Tamils & Rajasthanis. I rang *Ammi* to enquire about Abbu's health, but he was still taking rest. That day at work was quite hectic and arduous due to the many unexpected responsibilities that befell me. Therefore, even a petty task seemed quite challenging.

I arrived home at 9 PM. *Ammi* asked me to have dinner.

"How's Abbu now?" I asked her.

"Alhamdulillah, he is better now. Still, it will take a week or so as Dr. Manghani updated us today," she replied.

I didn't know what to say or how to react. Having had dinner, I slept early at around ten. That one day taught me the lesson that 'earning' was a tough battle. It was a race with a lot of uncertainty and risk on either side, but my confidence had grown thereafter. *Ammi* did not ask me about my day, as she was fussing over Abbu's wellness.

"We will have a special payer tomorrow," *Ammi* pronounced. She wanted us to offer an extra Namaaz for *Abbu* to get well sooner. We all agreed to wake up early at 4 AM the next morning. It was the time to connect with Allah in solitude and make our demands.

As discussed, we all offered this peculiar prayer one- by-one and beseeched for Abbu's good health.

After a week, I called up Dr. Manghani. "We need to speak with you. Can you please come over?" I requested him.

"I will not be able to make it immediately, but can we meet sometime in the evening?" he proposed. We agreed on meeting at 7 o'clock. Abbu had still not recovered even a bit, despite the doctor's reassurances.

"Someone is at the door," said my younger sister. It was the doctor with his briefcase in his hand. I ushered him to Abbu's room and he began the check-up. I updated him on his condition, and that he seemed to have forgotten us. I told him how he once called *Ammi,* but did not recognize her after a while. He seemed to have suffered a memory loss, but we could not give it a medical term. Even the doctor experienced it when Abbu failed to recognize him.

Abbu said to me, "Doctor, don't inject, don't inject, please," behaving like a school kid. It was really a piteous sight. I had forgotten how he used to be back in Mundka, and prayed to Allah to shower mercy upon him.

"Oh! Please take him to the hospital. I don't think I will be able to treat him anymore," the doctor said and stunned us all. We felt ripped apart. *Ammi* fainted without even knowing what the matter was.

"Doctor, what is it that you cannot do? Why do we have to get him admitted to a hospital? It is only typhoid, right?" I questioned. Meanwhile, my sisters shifted *Ammi* to another room and sprinkled some water on her face.

"Zaid, he does not have typhoid. It has developed into something else," he explained.

"What is this something else?" I retorted.

The doctor paused for a moment to gather his thoughts, then said, "Well, I suggest you rush to the hospital with him. They will make a better diagnosis for him."

Ammi regained her senses soon, but was most curious to know about Abbu. "What did doctor say?" she asked.

Considering her fragile state, I could not tell her the truth. "*Abbu* is fine," I told her. "We just need to consult a senior doctor at a good hospital," I fabricated. Dr. Manghani had suggested that we take him to Sri Ganga Ram Hospital in Rajinder Nagar, New Delhi. It was one of the most expensive hospitals in the country.

"Take him to Bara Hindu Rao hospital. It is a Govt. Hospital, so they won't charge much," *Ammi* suggested. This hospital was closer to our place of residence too.

"*Ammi*, you are concerned about the doctor's fee at this moment? Health always comes over wealth," I preached, though ineffectively. *Ammi* looked at my siblings to seek their opinion, but they stayed mum owing to their inexperience.

"I worry about his wealth and health both. He can get cured just as well in a govt. hospital. Such hospitals have great doctors. It is Allah who is going to heal him, not the doctors," she said, knocking me off with her words. She sounded illogical, albeit deeply passionate and emotional.

"Fine. Let's go to Bara Hindu Rao hospital," I commanded. My uncles already knew that Abbu had been ill due to typhoid, but I did not disturb them for going to the hospital. *Ammi* and I hired an auto rickshaw and took Abbu ourselves.

At the entrance of the hospital, Abbu suddenly turned to *Ammi* and asked, "Who are you?"

"I am Hajira, your wife," *Ammi* replied. "Who is Hajira?" asked Abbu.

"I am your wife, who has been with you for the past twenty years. Have you forgotten me?" she asked exasperatedly. Abbu could not remember anything, and remained lost in his own confused thoughts. *Ammi* asked me to get a glass of water for him, then poured it over his face. His face had become red from confusion and agony.

The security man at the entrance was watching all this. He got some more water and approached us to help. However, Abbu still refused to recognize both of us and got fiery and irritated. We knew that Abbu had turned a little soft since his illness, but this queer behavior and memory-loss certainly disturbed us. We did not know what to do, or what was wrong with him. We felt completely perplexed. We got to the emergency section somehow and sought a diagnosis for him. While Abbu was sitting on the bench, I said to him, "Asslamualaikum, I am Zaid!"

"Yeah, I am aware of that. Why do you have to introduce yourself to me?" enquired Abbu.

Ammi then told him how he had been behaving recently, refusing to recognize any of us. He refused to believe anything at first, then *Ammi* called that security man who confirmed having witnessed his erratic behaviour. He could not believe his ears, neither could recollect anything of the past few days.

"I don't want to see any doctor, let's go back home," Abbu insisted. *Ammi* sternly commanded him to stay, saying that she wanted him diagnosed thoroughly. A brief heated exchange between them followed.

"Let's go to the office," Abbu said to me while we were still in the hospital lobby. I was awestruck at his queer statements.

"Yes, we will go, Abbu," I replied. I sensed that he was feeling uneasy and wanted to puke, made apparent by his face and actions. We took him out of the hospital hurriedly, so he could purge. He felt relieved and smiled a bit after throwing up. We made him sit on a pew in the lawn outside the hospital. Many cars were parked nearby.

"That is my car. How do you like it?" he asked, pointing to a parked Honda City.

"Very nice," we replied.

"Only nice?" Abbu quipped. "It's a good car with all the features," he added proudly, as if the car were indeed his.

"Do you not recognize my car?" Abbu asked *Ammi*. "We do, and it's a nice car. We will go back home in it," *Ammi* said, looking visibly disturbed.

"It's strange that you both are holding me by your hands. You don't need to escort me," Abbu said irritatedly. We both were afraid that he would get even more sick if he continued rebuking us. It was now 6 PM and the wait was over! Our turn #55 which had been allotted to us almost an hour ago flashed on the screen and we went in to see Dr. S.K. Malik, M.D.(PSCHY), M.D.(Neuro), F.R.C.S.(London).

"Hello, Mr. Farooq. How are you?" asked Dr. Malik. "I am fit and fine!" replied Abbu.

"Then why are you here?"

"My wife wanted me to visit you. I am behaving awkwardly with my family apparently."

Ammi tried to intervene, but the doctor said, "Let me check what he has to say."

Abbu said, "I don't know but they think that I should be here…" He stopped speaking suddenly.

The doctor then asked *Ammi* to narrate what exactly had happened to him. *Ammi* told the doctor the whole story, right from when he had gotten the fever.

The doctor asked, "Is this the first time that you are observing such a queer behavior from him and his forgetfulness? For how long did he not recognize you or the family members?"

"Maybe one or two days," she said.

"Okay. I would suggest that you leave the patient with me for a while. You two may please take a seat outside," he said. We left the room, but I could hear them talking inside.

"Can you read this for me please?" asked Dr. Malik. "These are some sentences and pictures."

Abbu started reading, "These are the names of politicians...Pundi Jawa, Shustru, Zakaria Husna."

The doctor said, "Can you please read a little louder?"

Abbu was unable to understand what was written in the book. The doctor then asked him like a teacher asks a young child, "What is this?"

"It's a cat."

"What is that?" "That's a rat."

"Good, but rat is wrong. It is a pig, not a rat," said the doctor.

The doctor then called both *Ammi* and me back in his cabin. He said, "Mr. Farooq is showing early signs of Alzheimer's disease. He has a prominent clinical dementia, that's for sure. How old is he?"

"Forty-four years," replied *Ammi*.

"Well, it is rare to see this happening at this age. It has nothing to do with typhoid, but the sickness might have triggered the disposition. I do not want to scare you, but I suggest you get a blood test done along with an MRI and a CT scan. We will have a quick diagnosis of the patient. Please admit him into ward number sixteen, he needs rest. See me again once you get all the reports," said the doctor. We contacted the hospital reception for the same and had Abbu admitted there.

While he was hospitalized, many of our relatives visited him with fruits, juices and food items of his choice. Meanwhile, I travelling to Mundka by bus everyday and made sure that the business went on uninterrupted. *Ammi* took great care of him while he was at the hospital, changing his clothes, attending to all his needs, etc. Abbu was no better, and barely recognized most of the visitors.

A week later, I rushed to the city hospital to get the blood test reports along with the MRI and CT scan results. When all the reports were ready, I sought the doctor's appointment again.

"What do you think, doctor?" I asked Dr. Malik.

"What I was afraid of has indeed come true," he said. "His is a case of an early onset of Alzheimer's. Rather, too early! Given his health and age, it is very rare, but not impossible either."

I was stunned for a minute. I phoned *Ammi* upon leaving his office. "Abbu's reports are out," I told her, "and it is nothing serious. He will be fine," I lied. I was scared, but had to put up this façade so that she remained calm.

The doctor had told me that the grey matter of his cerebrum had started depleting, and his brain had shrunk. He was likely to lose his memory and slow down, sooner or later. His brain cells were dying, breaking the neurotransmission between them.

Ammi soon arrived at the hospital with my younger sister. I narrated the whole scenario to both of them. "How long will it take him to get better? It's been almost two weeks." *Ammi* said and burst into tears. My sister tried to pacify her and wiped her tears away. "Allah, have mercy on us!" *Ammi* sighed. I took them to meet the doctor who was just about to leave.

"Don't worry too much, he will be fine," the doctor told *Ammi*. "We will have to take utmost care of him, and not leave him alone anytime."

The good news was that his Alzheimer's disease was progressing quite slowly. The doctor told us that he would need a lot of care and personal sacrifice from his loved ones. We were absolutely disturbed but decided to take complete care of Abbu. Amidst all this, I had to look after the business as well, keeping the accountants from embezzling money.

Ammi's *Wazifa*

Two weeks had gone by and Abbu was back home now. The weather was changeable, alternatively cloudy and clear, but no signs of bad weather showed over the city of Mughlai food, art and culture. I wished for Abbu to enjoy all of it too. After many days he had remembered and addressed me by my name, much to the relief and happiness of all of us. *Ammi* had gone to my maternal grandma's house, which was about twenty kilometers out of the city. She was supposed to have been back by Monday, but it was now Thursday already. She never usually stayed there for more than a day.

"When will *Ammi* come back?" I asked my sister.

"I don't know, her Reliance phone is unreachable," she replied.

"But she said she would be back in a day, didn't she?" I asked.

"Yes, she did."

"You must have Naani's landline number. Will you please dial on it?" I asked. Our own landline telephone had been out of order for ages. I picked up Abbu's post- paid cell phone instead and asked my sister to dial my nani's number. Nobody picked up on the first ring, but it got through the second time and a girl received the call.

"Hello, I need to speak to *Ammi*," I said angrily.

"It's a call for *Ammi*," she called out on the other end.

My maternal aunt took the receiver now. I heard her voice after eight years or so. "Asslamualaikum, is *Ammi* there? She was supposed to be back on Monday evening. We are worried," I said.

"Walaikumasslam," she replied. "Your *Ammi* has gone out to meet Maulana Riyaz-ul-hasan, a renowned scholar and palmist here. He is only available from Monday to Friday." I felt a bit relaxed upon hearing this. "I will convey your message to her," she said and hung up. I had wanted to know more, as to when *Ammi* would return etc., but she had hung up before that. Villagers did not like to make long conversations over the phone usually. I tried dialling again, but could not get through. I figured that they had perhaps kept the speaker aside.

Back home, we all felt deeply anxious for Abbu at one hand, and for *Ammi* on the other.

"I want to eat some fruits!" A familiar voice rang through the room. Abbu was up. My siblings and I were amazed to see him uttering a complete sentence after weeks. We rushed to him.

"What would you like to have? Banana, mango, apple…"

"Grapes," he said feebly.

Unfortunately, we had only bananas at home, so I rushed out to get some grapes for him from a roadside vendor. We fed him some grapes and he smiled at us. It was a good sight, indeed.

"Abbu, please take rest," I said to him.

"No, it's too much! I have never rested so much in my life," he protested. I was afraid that if he talked any longer, he might feel uneasy. Knowing him, I knew that he never liked to repeat himself.

"Where's Hajira?" he asked curiously, as was typical of him. He never cared much for the rest of us anyway.

"She's in Meerut at Naani's house," I told him.

"Naani's house! Where's it? Where's Naani?" he asked in a shocking manner. I realized that he was having another attack of amnesia, made apparent by his queer expressions. My sister took out his medicines from the bed-side drawer. Abbu had them and went back to sleep. I found myself unable to handle the situation without *Ammi*, our angel and beacon of light.

I got a call from Gopal later that day, stating that there was a massive amount of work pending, since my attention had diverted to Abbu. I left for Mundka by a blue line bus, but kept thinking about Abbu and *Ammi* all through the journey. In that perplexed frame of mind, I reached my destination. It was brought to my notice there that Rashid had been irregular to work for quite some days. I called Gopal in to enquire about it further.

"What's wrong with Rashid? Why isn't he coming to work?"

"He told me that his sister is unwell, and he has to get her diagnosed. He is the eldest of all his siblings, so he feels responsible," Gopal replied assertively.

"Call him, I want to talk to him." I said. Gopal dialled his number, but it was switched off. He redialed, but to no avail. It pissed me off.

I got busy dealing with the suppliers who had been making rounds of the office to collect their payments. Both the accountants had been waiting for me to come and do it, yet a disturbed mind cannot lead. I wrapped everything up quickly and got back home by 8 PM. It had been a tiring day.

Things were no better at home as *Ammi* had not returned yet.

"When is *Ammi* coming back? Did you call her again?" I asked my sister, but only received silence in return. I wanted to see *Ammi* desperately, for she was the most important person in my life. Abbu's phone was getting charged by the window of the courtyard. I picked it up and dialled Naani's telephone number again.

"She will not come," proclaimed my sister.

"What?" I asked, shocked. "Why would she not return? What happened?"

"She will not return until Abbu gets well," she responded.

"What has Abbu's recovery got to do with her return? Rather, she should be back as soon as possible to look after him," I corrected her, but in vain.

"Maami called back in the evening and informed that *Ammi* has been advised by Maulana Riyaz-ul- hasan to employ certain holy verses from the Quran, by which Abbu will get absolutely fine," said my sister. I was dumbstruck. She had always sought my advice in all such matters. It was bizarre!

"How long is this practice going to take ?" I asked my sister.

"Well, Maami said that she is going to offer these prayers until Abbu gets thoroughly all right."

"What? Is she in her senses? This is crazy!" I hollered. With such practices as the norm, it felt as if something was wrong with me, and not them. 'What will happen next? What must the Maulana have advised? How long is all this going to take? She's *Ammi* and should have thought twice about her family before practicing spirituality,' I said to myself. It was perhaps foolish of me to think of *Ammi* as so immature. I hit the sack, even though these questions kept troubling me. My sister fed Abbu and gave him his medicines. We were all desperately waiting for *Ammi* to come back without any further delay.

"Zaid, where are you?" Abbu called out just them. I thought that he had slept.

"Yes, Abbu?" I responded, walking up to him. "Where's your *Ammi*?"

It was the most difficult question to answer and I did not wish to lie to him. "She has gone to get your medicines from a senior doctor," I regurgitated spontaneously, without a second of thought.

The following day, none of us could wake up at 5 AM, hence we all missed our morning prayers. *Ammi*'s absence had ruined our habit of rising up early with her. Since we had all slept late, all my siblings were still asleep even when the clock struck nine. Abbu was up but resting in his room. I was supposed to get ready for work, while dealing with a psychological battle inside. I could not imagine living without *Ammi* and eagerly anticipated her return. Thinking of all that, I walked up to Abbu and placed my hand on his forehead. I had never been so close to him since my childhood, because of the persistent tension between is.

"Are you fine, Abbu?" I asked him.

"Hmm," he smiled, then asked, "Where's your *Ammi*?"

I was in a flux, feeling exhilarated and greatly astonished at the same time. Abbu had never been so warm-hearted towards *Ammi*. "She is returning soon.

Do you want something to eat?" I asked, trying to distract him.

"When?" he asked directly. It certainly proved that he was still the father, and I the son.

"In a day or two," I responded, trying to give him some solace. Meanwhile, my sister came in and I asked her to prepare some breakfast instead of borrowing stress. While she went into the kitchen, I freshened up and got ready for work. After having breakfast, I headed out to catch a bus to Mundka.

'Will I always remain hedged around issues like this? Is my life ever going to get better? What will happen if something happened to Abbu?' Strange and terrifying thoughts did not leave me while I waited at the bus stop. It finally hit home, and I knew what to do. The bus arrived and I boarded, not for Mundka, but for Kashmiri Gate, Delhi. I wanted to get *Ammi* back, by any means possible. My Naani's house was in Kasha, one of the most backward villages of Uttar Pradesh. It was nearly 60 kms away from Delhi, and I hadn't been to that place in the last eight years. The bus dropped me at ISBT Kashmiri Gate at 10.15 AM. It was a huge depot of buses leading to different destinations across India. I searched for the bus bound to Meerut in the blistering heat.

"Meerut, Meerut, Meerut!" I heard a voice calling out from a distance, though I could barely see the bus. I chased after it and found the conductor marking tickets. People were in such a hurry to get in as if they had been exiled from the country with a death threat. It was horrible. I bought a ticket for twenty rupees and got in. Amidst all the hustle-bustle of sweaty passengers, I reached Meerut at 12.40 PM.

I felt famished and exhausted! There were *Tangas* (horse-drawn carriages) all around, reminiscent of the British era. I hired one to take me to Kashi. Upon reaching there, I saw naked children playing with mud, and buffaloes munching on fodder as usual. Unable to locate the house, I felt lost. It was the time of afternoon siesta in the village, and no one was to be seen on the street. A bunch of young children were playing with marbles on the road. I summoned one of them, but the entire group surrounded me, eying me suspiciously. They were all naked, dirty and inviting flies, but were least bothered about anything.

"Where's Mr. Ali Murtaza's house?" I asked, giving my maternal grandfather's name. They kept looking at me, but did not respond.

"We don't know," said one of them after a while and all of them started laughing.

While I was sweating under the sun, an old woman peeped through the door curtain of her house and took in the scene. As she came out, all the children dispersed immediately. She not only told me the address, but offered to go along with me. I finally reached my destination at 2 PM. The quiet and peaceful atmosphere of the village was a good change from the cacophony of the city and the travel. The house had fourteen people, including eight kids.

I entered the house and greeted my Naani, "Asslamualaikum." She was extremely pleased to see me and blessed me by stroking her hand over my forehead. I felt immediately transported to by blissful childhood when she used to shower her love upon all of us kids.

"Umm, where's *Ammi*?" I asked Naani, without losing another moment.

"She's in the *tehkhana* (lower cell/vault)."

"What's she doing there at this hour of the day?" I asked assertively.

"Don't disturb her! She is offering *Wazifa* (holy verses)," Naani warned me.

However, my curiosity knew no bounds. I just wanted to know if it had any relevance with what Abbu had been suffering from. "When is *Ammi* going to get free?" I persisted.

"In half an hour maybe. You must be tired, have some lunch," she offered.

Looking at the people there, I figured that they had no idea about the seriousness of Abbu's state. Everybody was quite chirpy and cheerful, which comforted me psychologically, but I didn't have any more patience. After having lunch, I retired for a quick nap on a cot under a tree, but there was no respite for me still. Nothing could pacify me. Naani came to me after a while with a platter of an assortment of sweets.

"I've prepared some sweets at home, try them," she offered.

I felt reluctant to accept them, and told her instead, "Naani, I will have it later. Can you please call *Ammi*?"

She kept mum, as expected. No sooner did she disappear, however, I sneaked down to the tehkhana. What I saw there was incredibly soul-filling. She was sitting, facing west–in the direction of Kabba Sharif[1]– deeply engrossed in prayer. I surmised that she must be directly linked to the creator spiritually, grounded in an untroubled venue.

1 A building at the center of Islam's most sacred mosque in Saudi Arabia

"Ammi, Ammi!" I called out. She remained motionless and unreceptive. I wondered if she was indeed my *Ammi*, cold-hearted as she was now. I tried again, drawing closer to her, but it was in vain. I felt lost and helpless, both with Abbu back in Delhi, and *Ammi* here in Meerut. I took a step back to return, taking in the dreamlike sight one last time. *Ammi* was right there in front of me, looking pale and hollow-cheeked. I sighed deeply as tears started to brim over my eye-lids. Seeing her again was the greatest treat I could ever have received from the heavens.

I believe in love at first sight, because I have loved *Ammi* since the moment I first opened my eyes to the world. I felt as if she had already unloaded my burdened soul. *Ammi* usually wore cotton tunics, mostly green and white. I noticed that she had on the same attire she left Delhi in. It was a green cotton suit, designating her the saint of our home. I held *Ammi*'s hand and kissed her divine palm. I deliberately bowed my head down so she could bless me, and she did. She probably felt more emotional than me in that moment. For a second, I thought she would burst into tears, but she was so lionhearted that all men had a lot to learn from her. The penury she grew up in and then Abbu's atrocities for twenty years had not broken her.

"*Ammi*, let's go back to Delhi! We have to take care of Abbu," I pleaded with her.

"I can't leave until he gets well," she insisted. "I have been instructed to offer exclusive prayers for your Abbu. It's a *mannat* (vow) with Allah. Hence, I can't move," she explained. I wondered how she would ever come to know whether Abbu was well or not back home, but his health seemed to be her first and foremost priority. I dug into my thoughts and philosophized why women were so accommodating and sacrificing for the sake of their husbands? Why wasn't it the other way round too?

"*Ammi*, let's go back. He has recovered remarkably since you came here," I said to give her hope, for she truly deserved it too. I wanted to shake off her adamancy in staying here.

"Is he able to recognize you all? I telephoned Nazia in the afternoon, she reported that there's no good sign yet." She was speaking the truth. Abbu had gotten better for sure, but had not completely recovered. I had exaggerated the situation, which did not fly. Time was ticking.

"Our lives are on hold without you there. We need to take good care of him. If you remain here, how will he get the much needed attention and care?" I pleaded. There was nobody else there to alter her mind besides me.

"I will culminate this spiritual course by tomorrow evening. We will then leave for Delhi," she reassured me. I broke into frenzy. I couldn't wait till tomorrow.

"Can't it be done at home in solitude, as per your convenience? We all are there," I tried to convince her, but she was adamant on performing the course that Maulana had instructed in the tehkhana only, as if it had turned into the most sacred place in the world.

I returned to Naani to seek her judgment on the issue, thinking that perhaps she would be able to persuade *Ammi* to go back, but she was of no help. I assumed that mothers had no control over their daughters once they became mothers themselves. However, I felt that my Maami was in favor of my attempts to get *Ammi* back. She didn't say anything overtly, but I read between the lines. Perhaps the privacy of her family life was getting interrupted by *Ammi*'s presence. I decided to capitalize on her intent and provoked, "Maami, why don't you make her understand? Shouldn't she come back with me?" I had taken the words right out of her mouth.

She rushed to *Ammi* and said, "Baaji, I think Zaid is right. You can accomplish the verses in Delhi as well." *Ammi* remained cautiously quiet.

"It's only a matter of two days. I have been meditating in the tehkhana for a week and it's a significant place for me now," *Ammi* upheld her view assertively.

Upon hearing the cacophony of voices in the house, neighbors started poring in one by one. I had witnessed this even in my childhood, all the neighbors with toddlers in their laps flocking my Naani's house uninvited. After having got an idea of the conversation, they all waited for their turn to contribute.

"Hajira, you should leave immediately. It's a wife responsibility to stand by her husband through thick and thin," said an old lady of about seventy five years. She carried weight in her words and *Ammi* paid attention to her and the other folks.

"Will it make a difference if I continue my prayers at home?" *Ammi* asked them.

"No, Allah is omnipresent!" said all, unanimously.

We decided to leave soon after. Fifteen women with their children accompanied us to the tonga stand bare- foot, where we bid them adieu. It was as if we were leaving on a pilgrimage. It was touching, to say the least. Amidst all the commotion, we reached back to Delhi around 6 in the evening. I couldn't shake off the recurring thought of why *Ammi* was so dedicatedly fussing over Abbu's health, despite his waspish attitude towards her for two decades.

When we reached home, *Ammi* headed straight for Abbu's room to check on his health, but he wasn't there. "Where's your Abbu?" *Ammi* asked Saif, my younger brother.

"He has gone out for an evening walk," he replied. I was standing outside at the washbasin, splashing my eyes clean which had consumed a bucket of dust. Saif's words struck me odd.

"Walk, and your Abbu?" *Ammi* pronounced ambivalently, mirroring my thoughts exactly.

"Yes *Ammi,* he got up himself and decided to go out," Saif said.

"Are you all right, Saif?" I asked in disbelief. This was miraculous.

"Yes, bhai. Absolutely."

"But, he was..." I floundered, not knowing what to say. This was finally some happy news after a long period of gloom. We eagerly waited for him to come back so we may look at him ourselves. I remembered how he had been writhing in pain just that morning, and wondered how he was even able to walk after that.

"He's gone out with Rizwan uncle," said Saif, as if he had read the questions in my mind. *Ammi* and I nodded.

Abbu came back after an hour, looking surprisingly bright. I was overjoyed to see him. *Ammi* had tears in her eyes, as did the rest of us. "How do you feel now?" she asked him after a week now.

"I'm very well," said Abbu. "Where have you been?" "I went to Kashi to give alms to the poor," she replied, concealing the truth. Abbu nodded. To everybody's surprise, he looked fit as a fiddle. It was an astonishing miracle. He recognized everything and everyone. We shifted to his room to continue talking.

I had a desire to speak with Maulana Riyaz and ask him what he had instructed *Ammi,* so I asked her, "*Ammi,* does the Maulana have a contact number."

"Yes, his telephone number is written in a diary kept in that drawer," she said, pointing to the bed-side drawer.

Five minutes later, I was dialling his number and spoke into the phone, "Asslamualaikum, this is Zaid, Mrs. Hajira Khatoon's son."

"The Maulana is busy with some patients," a female voice answered.

"Can you please get him on the phone for a minute?" I requested and she agreed.

"Hello Zaid, how are you?" Maulana asked in a cheerful manner upon taking the phone.

"I am well, and I have something important to share with you," I added.

"Your Abbu is fine now. Is that what you wanted to share with me?" he predicted. I smiled at his remarkable ability and felt unentitled to asked any further questions. He was a religious scholar and got his information through the spiritual route.

"Well, you already know," I said reverently. "Thank you very much, Maulana!"

"I did nothing. It was her passion to accomplish this herculean course flawlessly that matters more. My job is only to guide people," he replied. "Hat's off to your *Ammi*!" he said and hung up.

I couldn't thank Allah enough, I was at a loss of words. I realized that I couldn't have got a better mother than my *Ammi*. I looked up at the sky and smiled gratefully.

Delhi University

My physical and mental state got better over time as I got back to the same old regimented routine of going to Mundka with Abbu. Bad memories from the past had now gotten blurred in the wake of recent events and I thought it better not to antagonize it further. My acquiescence had much to do with *Ammi*'s ideology of blood being thicker than water too. Days grew seemingly serene and balanced, and I hoped for this time to never end. We were all pleased that Abbu, the patriarch of our house, was well again. In addition to that, he had stopped nagging us for petty things, taking on an indebted attitude over this time. I reckon it was due to all pains taken by *Ammi* throughout his illness. I wondered where all the uncles and aunts had vanished during those testing times for my family.

One evening, a bunch of plastic vendors flocked together to see Abbu while we were in the go-down. I guessed they must have come to check on his health. Abbu greeted all of them, while I kept preparing vouchers in the office along with Rashid and Gopal. Rashid went out after a while to get some tea, as it was well–understood and required no formal instructions.

"Farooq ji, when are you going to pay our interest?" a vendor asked. I had never seen this person before, nor did he own any factory in the market. I could hear their voices clearly.

"Let's sit at the main gate," Abbu said to the group softly. The group of five people, out of which I knew only two, got up from those untidy chairs at our office to leave. I didn't understand why Abbu couldn't converse in front of us. They carried their chairs down to the main gate, which was about fifty steps away from me. Now, I couldn't even overhear what they were talking about.

This sensation of missing out on something important overwhelmed me. Abbu's words had sounded queerly outlandish. I had only expected them to greet Abbu and ask about his health, which didn't happen surprisingly. I wondered what this interest was about. I was cognizant of the fact that parents often sacrificed for the sake of their kids, and there were certain secrets that they never shared, yet I found myself wanting to unfold this mystery of interest. Rashid and Gopal were my prime sources to target for information. The former was absorbed counting cash received from retail customers, while the latter was making journal entries in the ledger. However, I did not want to make an immature move, so I prudently decided to speak to *Ammi* about it first. I didn't intend to damage the newly repaired harmony in the family, particularly between Abbu and *Ammi*.

I saw those suppliers go back with no money in their hands or pockets. But the most noticeable were their dejected faces. The meeting had only lasted for about twenty minutes, unlike how it usually took hours with such company. While the sun was setting, we packed up to return home. The issue had begun to suffocate me, since we had already had a brawl with Abbu over the incurred debt of a million. While driving back, Abbu asked me how I was getting along with the business.

Considering that he might feel dishonored, I didn't ask him anything about the day's events. I got off the car near our house, carrying with me our lunch box and some cash. Abbu drove further down the road to look for a suitable parking space. I dashed towards home to consult *Ammi* over this matter.

"I got to know something really thrilling today. Abbu is supposed to pay back interest to some money lenders," I revealed to *Ammi*. She frowned at me for a while, as if I was giving her unnecessary trouble, trying to create a rift between Abbu and her.

"He is piling debt for us day-by-day. Where's the money getting utilized? We don't even study in public schools. Look, I don't even have a damn cell phone," I elaborated, anguishing. *Ammi* looked up at me in disbelief and irritation.

"I have no knowledge of this interest money. Also, it's forbidden in our religion. Why would he indulge in it?" asked *Ammi*.

"So, you don't know?" I confirmed. "No, I don't."

How was it possible that a spouse had no idea of something as deeply important as this? I didn't care to be circumspect anymore and revealed, "*Ammi*, I saw a host of money-lenders demanding money from Abbu today. There were frowning and did not seem very pleased with him."

While *Ammi* had known about the debt, she had not plucked up the courage to question Abbu about it yet. But our future was at stake now and I felt exceedingly solicitous about all of us. As far as I knew and had experienced, Abbu was relatively a skinflint. Where was he splurging then? Was there something wrong with his business strategies? Since I got no response from *Ammi*, I decided not to tell her anything anymore.

She was quick to notice my sour mood as I got up and ambled along the kitchen wall.

"What exactly do know about all this?" she asked, wiping off beads of sweat from her face.

"I am yet to dig in for more details. He has been quite tense since they visited. I thought perhaps you would know something," I replied, suggesting that she should remain more updated.

"Hmm, I see," she murmured. "We had him diagnosed and treated at a government hospital, and all of you study in government schools, then how come he is under such debt? Get some more information from Gopal and Rashid tomorrow," She suggested.

"Okay, I will."

I could think of various people to talk to regarding the matter, like Mr. Kartar Rajora–President of the Plastic Market Association, Rizwan uncle, and Tasleem Malik (Abbu's best friend). However, I pushed the matter to the back of my mind for the moment, since I didn't want to appear too big for my boots. Abbu came in just then, visibly exhausted. *Ammi* never initiated a conversation immediately on Abbu's arrival, but offered him a glass of chilled water and waited to let him get comfortable first. This was her attitude under all the circumstances. She never argued with him, partly for the sake of her kids' future and partly because of Abbu's volatile nature. So, we didn't talk about it any further and went to sleep as usual.

Upon reaching office the next day, I waited for an appropriate moment to accost Rashid and Gopal. They were crazily busy till late afternoon, as three consignments had arrived from Kota, Rajasthan. I got carried away with the flow of work too. Abbu entertained the suppliers with some tea and biscuits, while the entire staff and I were engrossed in reconciling the accounts. As they say, when you crave for something, it starts receding farther away from your reach. Whenever I looked up to see Abbu bursting into laughter with the suppliers, it gave me a strange feeling, knowing that he had an impossible pile of debt over his head. I felt particularly anxious because I knew that the debt would fall on me if he failed to pay it off himself. I was getting increasingly restless under the burden of anticipation, while both the accountants remained unaware of what I was going through. As always, I tried to keep the mood in office light, but everyone was under immense pressure from Abbu to finish everything by 5'o clock. The suppliers were to catch a train back to Kota after.

We came back home that night and *Ammi* greeted us with a smile. She called me into the kitchen to know if I had found out something to share with her. I told her to wait till the next day as it had been an extremely futile day at work.

The following day, I felt determined to find out who was Abbu taking money from. I couldn't let Abbu find out about my inquisitive research, not could I risk spoiling my rapport with the accountants by asking them suspicious questions about things they might not even be completely informed about. It had taken me ages to build their trust in me. It turned out to be a hectic day, selling the consignments we had received the previous day. I worked hard like an employee, which is just how everyone knew and treated me at office and the marketplace at large.

I constantly prayed for Rashid and Gopal to get free. At about five in the evening, I noticed Gopal ready to leave with his lunch box and ledgers in hand. I gestured at him to meet me at Saini's tea stall which was about ten meters from the go-down. He seemed to be in a hurry, but this had to be done.

"Gopal, who were those visitors yesterday who were demanding interest from Abbu?" I asked.

"They were the money lenders. Babuji borrowed 5 lacs on interest from them," he revealed. "But don't disclose it to anyone, please," he added.

I was nonplussed by the whole affair. I figured that he must have been cooking it for donkey's years since we hadn't got even the slightest idea of it. I dreamt of paying off a hundred crores to all the money lenders out of my pocket one day. A bleak future appeared imminent.

"I have to go now. Please don't let anybody know about it," said Gopal. He looked intimidated as he spoke to me in a trembling voice.

I thought of drawing more details out of Rashid to be doubly sure. I knew it would be tougher because of his unwavering loyalty for Abbu. Abbu had no clue about my sneaky endeavours, and seemed quite cheerful. I, on the other hand, detested his attitude. The more I expected to benefit from his name and lineage, the more disappointed

I got. He never let me drive his car, he was immune to my academic ventures, and he rarely showed any trust in me.

On our way home, Abbu asked me a few general questions about my progress in business as usual. He wanted to know if I was facing any particular challenges. I wished he knew what a challenge he had made life itself for us. Upon reaching home, I shared a detailed account of the happenings at work with *Ammi*.

"He will himself be responsible for all this. You don't need to be anxious!" she said.

"*Ammi*, he's ruining our careers, and his brothers won't bother pulling him out of this marsh," I explained.

"C'mon, he's your father. He must have thought things through for you." She just couldn't allege him for anything harmful.

One fine day, I witnessed a new bunch of people claiming their interest in a similar fashion from Abbu. I couldn't hear the exact figure of debt, but they definitely wore tough looks unsuitable for a small amount. I was determined to speak to Rashid now and find out if he had anything to add to Gopal's account of the situation.

"I want to speak to you. Meet me at Saini tea stall," I said to Rashid.

"Okay, I am coming in ten minutes," he replied. While I waited for him, I realized that he would most certainly spill the beans to Abbu, so I had to be careful in whatever I said to him.

"Yes, Zaid bhai. Tell me," he asked smiling, as he came down to Saini's.

"Who were those people who had come in the afternoon to claim some amount?" I asked.

"Umm...I don't really know," said he, reluctant to reveal anything.

"I won't disclose it to anybody else," I assured him, offering him a small bottle of soft-drink.

"No, I don't know anything about it. Perhaps Gopal would know more since he's been around longer than me," he said, evading still. I knew that he would rush to Abbu if I grilled him for information any further.

My investigation had proved futile, hence the last resort was Gopal again, even though I was unsure if he would reveal anything again. I was jovial to him all day so he would feel comfortable around me. That evening, I found him drawing lines on blank sheets to prepare suppliers' vouchers, which he was excellent at. Sensing that he would get very busy once he started calculating the number of consignments, I gestured at him to step out for a moment. I could see him barely enough in the light of dusk.

"Yes, Zaid bhai? What do you want to talk about?" Gopal asked, standing calmly. I wanted to put it to him with a sure tone.

"You must know the suppliers who visited Abbu this afternoon. How much is he to pay them?" I asked confidently. He smiled and his teeth, pearly white against his dark complexion, gleamed in the darkness.

"Zaid bhai, your Abbu has borrowed a huge amount of money from several money–lenders. The ones who came this afternoon were the *Chauhans*. They are very wealthy and powerful," he explained, looking hither and thither.

"Hmm, how much is he to pay them?" "About 20 lacs, I believe."

"Fuck! Where's all the bloody money getting invested?" I asked.

"I don't know that, honestly. But you may take a look at the ledger for a more accurate figure," he invited me to scan through the accounts. There was a candle lit at his desk, as it was post the scheduled 7 PM power-cut. He brought out a stack of papers from the almirah, which were scratched out all over. I requested him to aggregate the figure.

"It's 20,40,580," whispered Gopal. "Please, let it be between just the two of us. My job is at stake," he added. The fear was quite apparent on his sweaty face.

«Last question. Does Rashid know about this or not?" I asked, almost pleadingly.

"Oh! He knows everything, but he would never share it with anybody else," said he. There was indeed something that I was not aware of. I sank into deep daunting thoughts of the disaster that loomed ahead. What would happen if Abbu failed to pay back? How would *Ammi* feel? How would we all carve out our future?

When Abbu and I got home around nine in the night, we found some unexpected guests waiting for him at home. My *phupha,* paternal aunt's husband, and his brothers had come all the way from Hapur. The reason for their visit was yet unknown. I didn't quite like their presence in our house because of the complicated times that we were going through.

The paternal uncle was effervescently glad to see us. Perhaps he was hoping to have dinner with us. My *phuphi* – Shama Parveen had been married to him for fifteen years, yet they hadn't been blessed with a child, which is perhaps why the couple had plenty of time to indulge with their kith and kin, and show up at their houses at whatever time of the day or night. *Phupha* was extremely affluent and knew how to capitalize well on his inherited acres of land in Hapur. Unfortunately, he had always remained yearning for an offspring. God knew his mystery. This time, he had arrived with his younger brother.

"What are they doing here?" I asked *Ammi.*

"I don't know," she said, shrugging her shoulders.

I struck a conversation with him following after the Islamic greetings, all without any genuine interest though. *Ammi* spread a delectable Mughlai feast on the table for us, for which he grew quite cheerful. He was a hog for spicy food. He took his own sweet time to relish every bite, while I waited excruciatingly for them to wrap up dinner, so that

Ammi could ask Abbu regarding his debts. Neither *Ammi* not I made any eye- contact with Abbu throughout dinner. When they were finally done, *Ammi* went back into the kitchen to make some tea.

"So, Shehzad is getting married. Please accept our humble invitation for it. You all have to be there," Phubha proclaimed fervently.

'Oh, that's what this is about!' I said to myself.

He addressed only Abbu, for he knew that I might not be able to attend it. When *Ammi* returned with tea, he repeated the invitation to her, forcing a smile on his brother's face as well.

"Congratulations, Shehzad! Yes, we will certainly make it, inshallah," promised *Ammi*.

"You have to come at least four days before," *Phupha* insisted. *Ammi* smiled, but kept mum.

Abbu and *Phupha* got engrossed in their familial chit–chat, while *Ammi* cleared the table and returned to the kitchen. I barged into the kitchen after her.

"Is he mad or what? Is he going to stay around all night?" I asked *Ammi* out of frustration.

She simply laughed. "He's like that. You know how garrulous he is."

"*Ammi*, you need to ask Abbu about the debts as well. My interest in his business is growing thinner by the day because of this."

"Don't be so pessimistic, son. He will tell me the reason behind his debts," said *Ammi*, calming my adamant, yet solicitous, mind.

Phupha finally rose up to leave at half past midnight. He emphasized on the wedding date one more time, and we bid him and Shehzad goodbye. I wondered if *Ammi* would bring up the topic of Abbu's debt now, since it had already gotten too late. Yet, I could see the resolve clear on her face and guess what was to happen next.

"How's the business running these days?" she asked Abbu. It sounded queer at this hour, but Abbu was in a good mood, ready to face all odd questions.

"Yeah, alhamdulillah. It's going really well, and I have added some new clients from Chennai and Hyderabad recently," said Abbu, sounding ebullient and convincing. I settled myself behind the door of their room to overhear this conversation.

"That's good. I hope you haven't borrowed any money on interest," *Ammi* said, avoiding an eye contact with him.

"No, I haven't. Why would I?" Abbu answered.

"Hmm. We must not survive on that sort of money. It's forbidden in Islam and amounts to the unnecessary burden of paying back. We are happy in our modest ways. I don't want you or my kids to end up in a soup," *Ammi* added. I anticipated a great blow from Abbu in return, as it threatened to tip him over.

"Yes, I am fully aware of what's Halal (Permitted) and Haram (Prohibited) in Islam. I took some funds for Rizwan, as he was in a dire need of it," Abbu revealed, turning grimly serious all of a sudden.

"You are not responsible to meet his needs. He's self–sufficient enough," said *Ammi,* treading on very thin ice now.

"I didn't get him the funds willingly. It was all situational. He wanted to invest more capital in his business. That's it!" Abbu defended.

"Please educate him then that engaging in usury is a big sin, and Allah doesn't welcome it. It's tantamount to fornicating with your own mother, as stated in the scriptures," *Ammi* lashed out.

"I know all that and won't help him anymore," Abbu assured her conclusively. He wanted to get rid of this confrontation, as he left ridiculed by it. In hindsight, it must have been a great blow for Abbu. Thankfully, the conversation had taken place only between the two of them, otherwise it would have resulted in a higher degree of frustration. I didn't know if Abbu had genuinely taken money for Rizwan uncle, but his credibility was indeed at stake.

The next morning brought with it a lot of vacillation in me regarding going to Mundka. It began to scandalize me as I went to the mosque for the morning prayer at 5 AM, unable to disassociate myself from the financial jeopardy that surrounded us. A flood of thoughts ran through me as I turned to spirituality. How could I make *Ammi* understand Abbu's imprudent approach, the man who was unfairly biased towards his own children? He could go the extra mile for my uncles, but not for his own family. I wondered if I should stop going to Mundka with him? But if I did so, how would *Ammi* feel? My paternal uncles would hold me responsible for all the misdeeds carried on by Abbu. I will be made a scapegoat, I thought to myself. No sooner did the clock strike seven, I returned home.

My heart was pounding in rhythm with the wall- clock as I waited for *Ammi* to rise from sleep, so I could talk to her. She usually rested for an hour or so after the morning prayer. Meanwhile, I recited the holy Quran in my room.

"I need to speak to you," I said to *Ammi* as soon as she was up.

"Is there something new now?" she asked.

"I want to do something else, besides going to Mundka. There's nothing for me to do with Abbu."

"Oh! So you want to start from scratch?" *Ammi* asked sarcastically.

"Yes, I would," I answered, avoiding eye contact with her. I immediately imagined myself working my ass off somewhere at a petrol pump for a paltry amount. The thought did not intimidate me, for it seemed better than the wreck I was in at present. It was more satisfactory than living in a fool's paradise thinking that *Abbu* would reward me one day, or give me a pat on the back for having been a good helping hand to him.

"*Ammi*, my exams are approaching. I need to devote some time to studies as well now," I said, employing another technique.

"Show me the exam date sheet," she replied in a huff. I prayed to God to have my exams right away, so I could avoid going to Mundka.

"One of my classmates told me yesterday, our exams can be held any time. I haven't even unpacked the books yet, let alone look for coaching or tuition," I explained assertively.

"You don't want to continue working with your Abbu?" she asked. It was a tough question, though I didn't want it repeated.

"No, it's not that. I will continue it post my exams. The business will go on, but there's limited time for me to pursue academics," I expounded diplomatically. *Ammi* let it go, so I stayed back home that day. My primary aim for the day was to get an update on the exams. I knew *Ammi* would never let me squander away my time for too long, and the SOL correspondence office was just 2.5 kms from my residence, so I took a bus and went there the same day.

The campus was abuzz with students, some who had come to collect information, some to gawk at girls as if they had been assigned the task to identify the perpetrators behind a terrorist attack. I asked my way around to reach the SOL office. It felt like quite a task to switch over to study mode after so long, but beggars cannot be choosers, and I knew that well. There was a long queue at the information counter, and it seemed as if students from every corner of NCR had flocked there to get information.

I joined the queue at 1.30 PM, hoping that it would get shorter in an hour or so. To my dismay, it was lunch time for the staff, and I could see in through the windows–the dusty chairs, the lid-less water bottles and the sweaty handkerchief lying on the table. I asked a boy why the line was unmoving, and the students so passive and still. He told me if they broke the queue, the officials would shut the window and they would have to come back the next day. There were some rowdy students who could even murder others for the sake of their turn. It came as a great shock to me! These students had forgone their lunch, so did I. I could guess that it would take really long. I bumped into a bespectacled boy who was also in the same queue.

After mumbling a sorry, I asked him, "When are the exams going to commence?" It was humiliating for me to not be able to stand confidently before my equals. It is exactly what happens when you are made a factotum driven out of nasty circumstances.

"That's what I'm here for," said he, shooting his eyes brows at me. It was understandable, since we had been standing under such blistering summer heat, that too without food or drinking water, while drinking from the campus taps was below a student's dignity. I shut myself and didn't utter a word after.

The staff returned to their respective chairs, some holding a cup of tea. The queue proceeded at a snail's pace due to the despicable lethargy of the staff. I hated every moment of it and wanted to disappear somewhere. Mentally, I imagined raising up a revolution with all the students present there to kill the SOL staff, and have them replaced by younger, more passionate personnel. My turn finally arrived.

I peeped through the window at the enquiry officer and asked, "Sir, when do we have our B.Com exams?" He wore a check shirt, the breast pocket of which was torn off. It was an inapt sight, as far as Delhi University was concerned.

"Is it B.Com Pass or Honours?" he questioned back, a little annoyed.

"Oh! Sorry. It's B.Com Pass. I am very sorry," I replied nervously.

The students behind me were ready to run me over, like eagles scavenging for food. I maintained my composure and seriousness as if I had come to sign up for my Ph.D.

"The date sheet is not updated yet. You will get a correspondence from us very soon," he replied in haste.

'Bloody bastards, haven't even got the date sheet,' I said to myself. "Sir, is there a tentative date?" I asked him again.

He stared right into my eyes, his face a book of disgust and disgrace. "The first week of next month, tentatively. Now move along!" said he, irritated.

I vanished from the queue and took the first bus back home. This was the status of my academic life. Despite supporting my education myself, all I got in return was contempt from all directions. Yet, I had to find a way to get away from Mundka until the exams commenced. On reaching home, I racked my brains in an empty room. I knew *Ammi* wouldn't be pleased if I kept loitering around aimlessly. She never liked idles, and hated liars. Thankfully, I was not the latter.

Visit to the SOL Campus

"Hey buddy, have you purchased Champion books for the exams yet?" I heard a student ask another at the SOL campus. It sounded outlandish, partly because of my absence from the weekend classes conducted by DU, and partly because of not getting rightly counselled. It struck me then that I should have scored well enough to get admitted into a regular college. It was too late now. There were about half a million students who visited unresponsive, helpless and lethargic officials to get their queries sorted every semester. Nobody could revamp the structure; it was a vain hype for SOL created by the students themselves.

'Zaid, how will you nail it among so many jackals?' I asked myself. I had a premonition of imminent disaster. 'O Allah, please help me get through this difficult time, I prayed, looking up at the silent sky. I wanted to dig deeper into the Champion books enigma. They sounded like the hot topic of discussion on everyone's lips. While walking past the red bricked premises of the SOL, I glanced at some book vendors on the footpath, sitting behind tall piles of books – Neeraj, TOP & Champion as well. Everybody asked them for Champion books. The front page of each book was bright red with Champion written on it diagonally. I picked one up and scanned through it. It certainly broadened my smile, for the thickness of the book was easily conquerable. I could devour it overnight.

"Wow! Is this all we need to study in order to pass?" I asked the book seller, but he was busy entertaining other students. Another boy, who had heard my question, smiled responsively and said, "Yes, everybody studies from these books. We are not left with much time now anyway, so we will have to opt for this crash course," he explained.

"Do we not have other books like we used to in class 12th? There used to be sample papers, solved question banks and books from well known authors as well," I asked further.

"Oh bhai, nobody has the time to rack their brains over all that at the eleventh hour. If you wish to pass, study only Champion," he reassured me, as if he was a sales representative of Champion publishing house. I bought all five books of my course and rushed back home.

It was high afternoon and I tried to settle for a snooze.

"Have you got your exam date sheet yet?" *Ammi* enquired.

"Not yet, it will be circulated in a day or two," I replied.

"Are you sure?"

Well, yes. I met a couple of intelligent students at college today, they told me so," I lied.

"Okay. If there's any delay, you should join your Abbu back in his work. You have been loitering idly for quite a while," said *Ammi*, turning bitter. I didn't respond.

A guilty conscience needs no accuser. I could happily have been employed at a cobbler's kiosk and polished boots, but not return to Abbu's business, yet I remained silent.

A week passed. I got engrossed in the exam preparation. Cr*Ammi*ng up from all those books was no big deal. I made a visit to the SOL office again to get an update on the exam schedule, and was surprised to find the exam date sheet for all DU courses stuck on the walls. They had apparently been there for about three days already.

Financial Accounting – 3rd June English – 5th June

Economics – 8th June

Business studies – 10th June Urdu -13th June

On one hand, I was relieved that I had some concrete information to confidently share with *Ammi*, while on the other hand, I felt nervous about doing well in the exams. Besides, some senior students from B.Com 2nd year had terrified me about getting a low percentage at SOL.

They said, "No matter what you do, they always award you with a 45%. Only about 5% of the total students scored 60% and above in the last year exams." It had sounded rather ridiculous to me, but I wished to talk to a veteran teacher about it, just to be sure of how to go about studying.

I bumped into a teacher behind the canteen that very day. "Sir, may I borrow a minute?" I interrupted him. He was counselling some equally curious students who stood in a group around him.

"Yes, tell me?" he looked up and waited for me to speak.

"Sir, is it true that students can only score upto 40 to 45% at SOL?"

Everybody, except the teacher, giggled. It was a brush–off for me. I couldn't quite understand whether it was good or bad.

"Son, it is not like that. Anyone who works hard will be rewarded," said the teacher in an idealistic tone. I wished I was mature enough to know what to ask and what not. After being humiliated such, I slipped away. I wondered if the books back home were enough for me to score well. I wanted to reshape and break through that 40% convention, even though I knew it was easier said than done. I always felt inspired by the words of educationists, but it never lasted for more than a day or two. I got a bee in the bonnet, but let it fly out shortly. *Ammi* was relieved that my exams finally had a definitive schedule. I secluded myself and retired to my room to study.

It was finally time for me to steer through all odds and stand up to the mighty expectations of my *Ammi* and Abbu. I knew he would annihilate me if I didn't do well, as he was concerned only with the results and not the process. SOL always held exams in May/June, which was unfortunate because students were forced to find their examination centers in the blistering heat of summer afternoons.

On 3rd June, I set out to write my first exam. Restlessly, I scanned through the seating-arrangement chart and reached my desk just in time for the bell. The classroom was entirely populated by boys, as the girls in the batch had already sat for the paper that morning in another shift.

"Ah! There is no chick," muttered a guy from the back of the room and everybody laughed. Clearly, priorities had been outlined even in the most anxious of situations. I prayed to the Almighty one last time before the invigilator handed me the question paper. I partially knew most of the questions, but did not feel fully confident in any. I resorted to filling the pages with rubbish answers, as I had been doing since class five. I pretended to be highly serious, but my frequent pauses, ticking of the pen, wiping the sweat and chewing on the pen's cap said it all.

The invigilator looked like a hawk-eyed scientist who'd drop an atom bomb over whoever attempted to cheat, though I couldn't even dare to look to my side. As the final bell rang, all the boys submitted their answer scripts one after the other and moved out of the classroom.

I didn't chat with anybody, but just boarded the bus to go back home. I hoped that *Ammi* would pray for my success in this exam. It was unusual for me to attempt five questions of twenty marks each. It was way different from the CBSE exams I had taken before. I had no hint about the appropriate length of my answers. It was simply 'd*o well and forget'* policy for me.

"How was your exam?" *Ammi* asked.

"Huh?" I was still too absorbed in rewriting my answers mentally.

"Yeah, it was okay," I replied.

"Only okay?" *Ammi* asked, startled, as if I was meant to outdo the entire DU campus.

"Hmm, it was tough. Plus, that bloody invigilator was too strict," I said, throwing off the blame.

"Okay. Don't worry, you will get through it, inshallah."

The warmth in her words was so comforting that I didn't even feel like eating anything. It had an instant healing effect over me, dissipating all my worries in an instant. Thereafter, I went in to write my exams more courageously and finally took a deep sigh of relief on 13th of June.

A week went by, and my laxity and idleness started pinching my parents. It was unbearable for them to see me glued to the TV for drama soaps and India v/s Pakistan test series. I wanted to let it go on like this forever. I even fancied having delicious food throughout my life without having to do any hard work at all, or at least, by not engaging in Abbu's business. But fate had the reverse in store for me.

Abbu returned from Mundka at 9 PM that night as usual. He entered the living room with a scowl on his face, while I was watching TV. He screamed, "You bloody indolent boy, why don't you move your ass and work with me? I can't see you pigging off food all the time." I looked around to find ways to evade further confrontation, but it was in vain. "Now that your exams have gotten over, what are you going to do?" he asked with a frightening look.

My throat went dry with fear. "I am going to resume my tuition classes. There are five students who have been wanting to study," I said, my head bent low.

"Good! Have you already started?" "No, I am going to."

"Okay. If that's what you want to do, go ahead then."

I was over the moon with his official consent. I wondered how this escape had come along so easily. He would never let me venture out freely, but this time, there wasn't even a tinge of resentment in him. *Ammi* later apprised me of the truth.

"He feels insecure as you tend to peek into his accounts and transactions. There're things that require him alone, not you. It's his empire, erected by virtue of his own dedication, passion and infinite hard work. Therefore, you may start teaching students, but…" she paused.

"But what?" I asked.

"Your earnings should be spent on the family, and he would have it accounted as well," she elaborated. I listened, mouth agape with incredulity.

"*Ammi,* I haven't even started yet. His expectations are unfair," I defended. This task seemed even tougher than working with Abbu. I did want to contribute to my family, especially *Ammi,* but certain factors were out of my control, like my success with teaching. Though I was a small fry, there were extremely high expectations of me. I could visualize him taking pleasure in lashing out at me, for not having adhered to what he had dictated. *Ammi* encouraged me to start teaching as soon as possible, capitalising on every passing moment. I was certainly offending her with my lethargy. After a while, I seriously started hunting for learners in my vicinity. I contacted a few parents as well. I recounted to them my previous stint at teaching and the great success that it turned out to be. I even prepared a pamphlet to advertise it.

A cyber café owner helped me with it and I got fifty copies made of a printed advertisement. Clutching them in my hand, I approached some nearby newspaper vendors and requested them to drop the pamphlets at residents' door steps along with the newspapers.

"Sir ji, many parents are looking for good tutors. In fact, a woman was asking me about one just yesterday," a vendor told me. I got instantly intrigued, and asked him who the woman was, slightly blinded by hopeful delusions.

"She has two small kids who study in Navbharti School. If you want, I will talk to her," he said.

I was impressed by his interest and helpfulness. He had laid the foundation for me already. I wondered if he would actually be able to get students for me. I left no stone unturned myself, as I got even the street children to spread the pamphlets at the local mosque, with the promise of treating them with tandoori chicken and Coca-cola in return. There were as many street urchins in my locality as the total population of Sri Lanka, or so it seemed by their hullabaloo all day. I imagined myself getting popular amidst the huge congregation of devotees as they flocked the mosques, all with my poor word-format pamphlets!

Back home, *Ammi*'s concern was mounting up. She had asked me a couple of times what my plans were. I simply said, "Inshallah! Please pray for me." Everything was still in the pipeline. I used 'Inshallah'– if the Almighty wishes, as a weapon to assuage my attackers, as they couldn't counter it.

The next morning, I rushed to the newspaper vendor to get an update on my prospective students. It was six in the morning and there were hardly any buyers there. He had his shop set up on the footpath. It was a precarious situation for me, given the ultimatums given to me at home. He arrived on his bicycle with a stack of freshly pressed papers on the carrier behind him.

Luckily, he recognized me and said proactively, "Bhaiya, she will contact you today. I've shared your telephone number with her."

"That's good. Thank you," I grinned gratefully, not knowing the price I was going to pay for it.

"What will I get in return?" he asked, smiling slyly.

I was absolutely stunned. "What do you need?" I asked.

"Well, you are a teacher. You understand everything," he said, laughing. "Bhaiya, give me a hundred bucks on every student I send to you," he added.

I watched him in disbelief. 'Zaid, if you need to establish a tuition center, you will have to grease his palms initially. That's how the world is,' said my inner voice. At once, just to shut him up, I agreed.

I constantly kept checking with the children and the newspaper vendor if they had met any prospective learners for me, but no news was good news. I had to put up pretences for *Ammi* now, so I picked up my Economics guide and sat in a separate room. I either held the books in my hands or let them rest upon my folded legs in the shape of Rahal (Quran holder). I managed to win back *Ammi*'s confidence.

Yet, only after about two days, I could see a conspicuous concern on *Ammi*'s face. She firmly believed that there was a time for everything, and if I lost this opportunity to make something out of myself in my youth, I would not be able to succeed for the rest of my life. My heart swung in the opposite direction, however. Somewhere deep inside, I also wished to fall for someone, I wished for a girl to long for me, or vice versa.

I would step out only for Namaaz and remained confined with my books. Restlessness engulfed me as I was not getting approached by any students or parents even after a week. It had now become necessary to proactively speak to *Ammi* about it. At around 5 PM, I entered *Ammi*'s room. She was just settling down to read the holy Quran. She must have read through my tormented state when I entered. She sat on our old single bed, while I opted to sit on the floor by her feet.

Her gaze was curious, anxious and tense. I summoned the courage to finally speak, "I'm not getting any responses for the tuition. I have tried my level best," I broke the news to her.

She turned more attentive than ever. I could see tears welling up in her benevolent eyes. I was stunned and repented saying the words.

"Inshallah, you will have many students. Don't give up!" *Ammi* said palliatively. This was the encouragement I had been looking for. "Keep trying and never lose hope in the mercy of Allah. But don't think you can sit idle and leave everything upon Allah. You have to make the attempt. That's what Allah mentions in the holy Quran," she smiled and the entire burden just dissipated in an instant. I wished I could crown her worthy of the entire wealth of this planet.

The night welcomed me with sound sleep, while I kept *Ammi*'s words in my mind. It struck me that I would be able to survive under her shelter for a few more days, or as long as I could save myself from Abbu's inquisitive eye.

While taking ablution in the mosque one day, I heard a resident, about forty years of age, from a nearby locality talking aloud to two other people. His face was grim but not rude. "You must give alms to the needy, it makes the mare go," the man said. I had otherwise been hearing that money makes the mare go. The story was reversed in this instance. "This is what Allah likes the most," he added with conviction.

"If somebody does not have enough to offer, then?" asked a curious listener. I too was yearning to put a similar question across.

"One can contribute even a rupee or a fruit. It's all about intent and faith," the man explained. I drew closer to have him understand my situation.

"What shall I do to succeed? I want to become a teacher," I asked, indiscreet.

"What did you say?" he asked, looking me up and down. I repeated myself, emphasising on 'success'.

-"Yes, there's a sure shot way to succeed through the spiritual channels. Have a transaction with the Almighty."

"Transact with the Almighty? What do you mean?" "We are all his slaves. If you help anyone of us,

Allah will be pleased and you will be bestowed with the best."

"How may I contribute?"

"Alleviate people's plight by any means." "Can I do it without money?"

"Of course, you can. Do anything that brings a smile in people's lives," he elaborated with a gentle smile. His words began to steer through my cerebral channels. I, of course, had nothing to lose. Investing in the needy thus seemed appropriate. If I could please the omnipotent, it would get me going. A sense of determination took birth in me to positively take a step in that direction. I thought of talking to *Ammi* about it, who grew pink upon hearing such nobility from me. She suggested I began with feeding the needy.

The next day, she cooked a pot full of rice and daal for me to take to the mosque. A bunch of beggars and street urchins followed me upon seeing the pots. My cheerful smile manifested all my noble intentions, so I let the bunch follow behind me. When I reached the mosque, some people immediately came to my help to unload and serve. Divinity had already begun to shower upon me. I recognized His kindness in the form of those helping hands which came to feed the needy.

I reiterated the teachings I had received at the Madrasa in my childhood.

"Get close to Allah before getting close to anyone else; Allah without a man is still Allah, but a man without Allah is nothing."

"People will forget a thousand good deeds done by us for one fault. Allah will forgive a thousand bad deeds for a good one."

Sometimes, the whole life can be summarized in a few words. We invited all the people into the courtyard of the masjid, and helped them sit on the floor. Smiling faces beamed graciously at me. Two of us put the food into plates, while one looked after the quantity in the pots. Everyone looked warm and happy. They relished every bite, as if it was a source of solace. The sun finally set with no darkness behind.

The much anticipated result manifested quite instantly, as somebody rang at my home telephone for a query that very day. Later that day, I learnt from *Ammi* that a married couple was waiting for me in the drawing room. I was overjoyed and rushed to attend to them. The man greeted me, "Asslamualaikum, sir."

I sprang up at 'Sir'. It was hard to believe my ears. He must have been in his 40s. He wore a green embroidered kurta and white pajamas, and his wife was in a burqa. She didn't talk much, but kept nodding to what her husband said.

"So, how many kids are you blessed with?" I asked, smiling.

"Sir, we have two. A son–Ayaan, and a daughter– Farah."

"Which school do they attend?"

"Sir, they're in Navyug School, Birla Mandir."

"Please, don't call me *sir,*" I requested. Although, it did make me feel like on top of the world inside.

"Sir…" the lady attempted to speak.

"Yes, go ahead," I encouraged her, offering her a glass of water.

"Actually, it is we who want to study English, not our kids."

"Oh, really?"

"Yes, sir. We would request you to kindly keep our request discreet," the couple pleaded. A tinge of embarrassment appeared clear on their faces. In hindsight, I shouldn't have just sat there, jaw-dropped, as perhaps it made them even more uncomfortable.

Yet, time teaches what nobody can. Things were unfolding beyond my imagination. People had begun to notice my tiny efforts in the direction of my passion. Success was finally knocking at my door. It was totally unbelievable. I kick-started my journey as a tutor again with those shy parents. They would come for the classes in the afternoon. Before teaching them, I had to study for an hour or so to be completely confident. Interestingly, there was no one to guide me through. Neither could I afford a tutor, due to financial constraints. As they say, necessity is the mother of invention, and invent my own skill, I did.

Fleeing From Home

Abbu was doing well in his den, while I was gradually making my presence felt too. There were more students than ever at the my coaching set-up at home. *Ammi* was pleased to see the response and always welcomed the learners warmly. She would make them sit in our drawing room and offer a glass of water to make them feel at home. It was her endeavor to fortify my occupation from all fronts. I failed to understand why she always emphasized upon employment, while it was not the case with my aunties and other relatives for their kids. More often than not, they only flaunted their hollow splendor. As for me, I was barely making 2200/- rupees a month, not even 1% of what Abbu was generating in his business. In hindsight, Abbu was never convinced with my teaching stint and the peanuts I got from it. He often questioned me about the number of students I taught and the fee I drew from them.

I was particularly observant of how vaguely our clan displayed personal wealth, and how hollow it all was. No one had ever come to understand the reason behind the illiteracy prevailing in the whole clan of nearly seventy folk. All my siblings and I went unnoticed due to our unostentatious way of life.

As things began to settle for me, I thought of expanding my coaching classes by convincing my existing students to publicize it by word of mouth. They also seemed quite affirmative of my strange mission. They'd become my strength and catharsis against my father's judgement of me.

One evening, I was teaching a bunch of students when I saw Abbu coming back from Mundka. He looked fatigued and extremely pissed, made apparent by his face. I tried to make eye contact with him but he avoided it. I didn't deliberate over it as he had always been like this. "You ought to smile while at home," says Islam, but we had only inherited the reverse of every islamic value from him. I intuited that something bad was about to go down. I busied myself in teaching, pretending not to have noticed him. I wished to remain out of his way for the rest of the night, so he wouldn't ask me any questions. He had his meal quietly and went out for a stroll.

"Where's Abbu gone?" I asked *Ammi*.

"I don't know, perhaps for Namaaz," *Ammi* shrugged. Whatever it might have been, I simply heaved a sigh of relief. It terrified me at times to even have a conversation with Abbu, while being forced to look into his eyes. He was *Abbu,* yet we had never shared even a baseline of comfort with each other. The thought of spending even a minute with him invited goosebumps and made my adrenaline spike up. I had pined for his affection and fatherly love throughout my life, but it was *Ammi* who had always insisted upon us to endure and inculcate a *grin and bear* attitude. She bore all the lows of life with cheer, though I felt appalled at this. I often thought how a person could be so obedient and patient for someone who had brought so much disgust to her and her kids on innumerable occasions.

I was having dinner when Abbu came back. Everybody at home turned dead silent suddenly, as if under the red alert of a war zone.

"Allah, have mercy!" I sighed mentally. While his presence was detestable, I could not imagine living without Abbu either. I could not turn against him because I did not have the strength to stand against our huge clan which could obliterate me in seconds. I knew that if Abbu turned against *Ammi* because of me, we stood no chance of survival.

" Asslamualaikum," I said to Abbu.

"Walaikumasslam," he replied sternly, to no surprise of me or my family. "Get me some water, Hajira," he commanded. He drank from the silver pot of water, then kept it aside. I had slowed down my pace of eating, terrified by his proximity. I anticipated that he would punch me in the face today.

"How many students have you got now?" he asked, looking into my eyes. I wondered if he expected me to grow the numbers by seconds.

"There're twelve at the moment. Also, I got an enquiry from three boys who will hopefully join soon, *inshallah*," I responded.

He turned bitter and I could see his resentment turning into fire balls in his eyes.

WHACK! WHACK! WHACK!

He smacked me thrice on my cheeks, partially hitting me in the eyes too. *Ammi* and my siblings kept looking at him, but stayed away. I wanted to retort, 'What the hell do you want out of me? I'm not a superman!' but kept mum. He looked at me in a furious manner, but I kept my gaze locked on the floor, also cracked like me. Never had he been logical in his beatings, whether it was *Ammi* or I as the victim. He simply bashed us ceaselessly, ridiculously and mercilessly.

"How much are you earning these days?" He thundered. I shuddered as my courage had been thoroughly shaken and couldn't answer him immediately. "Will you say something or not? I'll tan his skin, Hajira," he roared, yanking *Ammi* now. *Ammi* looked at me so I would answer.

"Rs. 2,200/- a month," I said, sobbing.

WHACK! WHACK! He smacked again. It was more painful this time. My left cheek had turned crimson.

"Beat him more, beat him to death!" cried *Ammi*. I knew that she had gotten fed up with this. I wished I could alleviate her agony, but felt helpless in the situation.

"You earn peanuts, you bloody swine! Why can't you earn in lacs?" He added salt. Neither I nor *Ammi* understood what he wanted from us. He had never been happy with me at his go-down, and was now creating this drama with regard to my coaching as well. I longed to understand why I took birth at all.

Abbu put on his slippers and stepped out. Perhaps he had gone to meet his brothers to share what he'd rewarded me with. Beating me was his catharsis which he could bank on anytime. As a ritual, we all got together and consoled each other. *Ammi* was my best comfort, of course. A little later, she wept miserably in the other room. What could I do except hoping that something redeeming would happen someday. We lamented the atrocities done upon us by Abbu and wondered if it would ever end. We all only had a voice in the company of each other where we could speak our minds without the fear of rebuke or violence. It was 1 AM when we finally slept. We anticipated that Abbu would not return home that night, but he did.

"What time did he get home last night? " I asked *Ammi* the next morning.

I had deliberately stopped referring to *Abbu* as Abbu, and resorted to a unassuming 'He'. As expected, I couldn't let it fly for too long.

"Who's he to you?" *Ammi* questioned me, raging. I hadn't expected this even in my wildest dreams.

"My father!" I said, frowning.

"So, call him Abbu," she added.

"Despite all his barbarism and outrage?" I defended. "Yes, even then you're to do it. By the way, you're a *hafiz* (an Islamic scholar). You need no enlightenment on this," she said sarcastically.

I felt stunned for a moment. "Enough is enough! He's also a *Maulvi* (a scholar of a lofty stature). Is this how he's supposed to behave? Is this what Allah commands in the Holy Quran? Is this how Prophet Muhammad (peace be upon him) used to interact with his wives and children?" I spewed out my toxic anger.

Beads of sweat appeared on her forehead, but she remained word-less. She hurriedly headed for the kitchen and said evasively, "He's not going to be held accountable for all your deeds. He will sleep in his grave and the Law of the Lord for Judgment Day is quite stringent."

I wanted *Ammi* to maintain eye contact with me while she spoke, so I followed after her and said, "Are all the rules of *Sharia* (Islamic jurisprudence) only applicable on me?"

"You're a child, okay. Don't debate!" she warned me.

"Okay, I agree," I said in an attempt to appease her. "Now tell me, what time did Abbu come?"

"At 3.30 AM," she said. I was sure that *Ammi* wouldn't have slept at all the previous night. She must've stayed awake to open the door like an unpaid

guard. I had often wondered it this happened in every Muslim family, because it appeared to touch the heights of ludicrousness.

Abbu was having breakfast in the drawing room then. Due to the previous night's drama, none of us sat near him. Nonetheless, he was absolutely happy being alone. I wondered how low a parent could go in the way he dealt with his child. While he expected to see me do wonders, he never guided me through nor appreciated my tiny strides. Never had he expressed an interest in my future to *Ammi*.

"*Ammi*, why does he never appreciate me?" I asked. "You've started it again! You're pissing me off," she dodged the question.

"You know how much it already pains me to see him showering all his love and blessings over his nieces and nephews," I unloaded my frustration, walking towards the washroom.

"However he may be, you still have to respect him," she reinforced adamantly.

A little later, Abbu cruised off to his calling without a word to either *Ammi* or us. He was entirely unreflective and unrepentant of his egregious behaviour with us.

It was 1 PM and my first batch of students was about to arrive. I didn't feel like doing anything and told *Ammi* I didn't feel like teaching that day, but she never let anything get in the way of my meagre means of income.

"Beta, don't lose heart! This is a phase of learning and you'll remember it," she reiterated. I felt thankful that at least she didn't want me to take over Abbu's business anymore. We had been disillusioned of that hope. I didn't argue anymore and slammed the washroom door shut behind me to take a shower.

Ammi went to the terrace to put the laundry out to dry over a clothing line that she had set up there herself. I came out after the shower and changed into a white kurta pyjama that I usually wore at home.

"Have the students come yet?"*Ammi* shouted from the terrace. She had never been to school herself, yet her love for academics and teaching was incomparable.

"Not yet, *Ammi,*" I replied. The clock was ticking away, but nobody showed up. This was happening for the first time since I had started teaching.

"You must be so pleased that they've not come," said *Ammi*.

"No, not all," I lied.

"Beta, I'm your mother. This is what you wished for, I know," she added further.

"No, it's not like that," I defended myself, as though I was on trial.

"Why don't you phone any of them?" *Ammi* suggested.

"It's already three, there is no point in it," I said.

"Don't flinch away from your living. It's by Allah's blessings that you've kick started your coaching so early.

You'll have uncountable students one day, inshallah," *Ammi* blessed me. Her words seemed surreal. I had always been a barely average student in school myself, yet here I was teaching others. It was the joke of the century!

The next day onwards, I got back mechanically to my schedule of living and dealing with despicable circumstances. I taught my students as usual, but my enthusiasm had certainly dissipated away. I didn't want to expand my classes any longer. I felt content with the existing number of students I had. The reason was not lethargy or a lack of ambition or vision, but because I had lost the belief in the longevity of my existence. *What if I never wake up tomorrow?* A weird web of such thoughts nabbed me from all corners and filled me with chagrin. I also flirted with the idea to running away from home.

It was Friday and I showered early in the morning to join the *Jumma* (Friday) *Prayer* with all my childhood chums. The community prayer meet up was a great way to catch up with all those whom I couldn't see the entire week. There were around four hundred believers and some beggars in the mosque. Begging is a major sin in Islam, yet no reformative action was taken to mitigate their poverty. The prayer began with an Arabic preaching which lasted for fifteen minutes. After that, we all stood up to offer a five minute prayer. I stepped out of the mosque and talked to a couple of my friends who were eating Chicken Biryani just at the gate of the mosque. Most of them gathered more keenly every Friday only to have a gastronomical ride. I had some bites and came back home, turning a deaf ear to my friends pleading for me to stay.

Ammi offered me lunch. I took rest for a while, as was customary. In my mind, however, I was thinking of running away that very night to make Abbu realize my importance. I had some cash, not more than a hundred rupees, from the fee I had recently collected from the students, the rest being deposited with *Ammi*. I wanted to leave the house before Abbu came back. I finally decided to go to ISBT, Delhi.

I walked on foot all the way from my residence to Kashmiri Gate, just to save as much money as I could. The sight of multiple busses leaving for a diverse set of destinations–Uttar Pradesh, Rajasthan, Himachal Pradesh, Madhya Pradesh, Haryana and Punjab, all seemed like my ticket to freedom. I wished to be anywhere but back home. The conductors were screaming amidst all the smoke from the exhaust pipes. Sweaty passengers crowded the terminus with young kids eyeing the attractive but unhygienic eatables– coconuts, toffees, grams and puffed balls–that the hawkers were selling

I made up my mind to board the Punjab Roadways bus without giving it a second thought. I had never been to another city before, but there is a first time for everything.

"Where do you want to go, *jawaan*?" asked the conductor. He must've been in his sixties, and was wearing a work out plaid shirt and trousers. He looked extremely happy with his job, and had a contagious smile on his face. It changed my mood and made me wonder how he could be so satisfied with a job that could not have been offering him more than 5-6k. It gave me hope and I said to myself, "Zaid, you can excel too."

Upon spending a week in Ludhiana, I got employed at a Punjabi *dhaba*. My job entailed serving and purchasing raw materials from a nearby market called Lalu Bazar. Surinder Pal Singh, also known as Ladi Paji, was the owner of the dhaba and would've hired me for cleaning if it had not been for my good looks. He was gracious enough to help me in such a tight situation. I would sleep at the dhaba around 1.30 AM, wake up at 6 AM sharp to go purchase the vegetables and meat. I then got so occupied throughout the day that nobody knocked at my memories except *Ammi*. I missed her all the time. It had been a week since I had last heard her say, "Zaid, have your food and sleep!" I wore the same clothes, jeans and an orange T shirt, that I had brought from home everyday. I hadn't carried anything with me that was bought by Abbu.

I often wondered what must be happening back home, and if my family or clan thought of me at all. I wondered what Abbu would be doing. The guests at the dhaba often mistook me for the owner's son, or a part-timer, since I looked far better than my situation. At the same time, I fought the dilemma of sticking around or not.

One day, an old man who appeared to be in his 70s entered the dhaba. He was dressed neatly in a white shirt and black pants, and was clean shaven and groomed. Never had I spotted such a gentleman at the dhaba before. I sped up to him to get his order. He smiled at me, and I reciprocated it.

"Sir, what shall I bring for you?" I asked.

"Are you responsible for taking orders here?" he quizzed, nonplussed.

"Yes, I am."

"What brought you here? You look like a college student." His words hit me like a bull in the wall.

"It's nothing, sir," I attempted to remain casual and continued serving the other guests.

The sun was setting once again, and I felt a Sisyphean exhaustion. The gentleman held me back by my arm to talk to me and maintained an unwavering eye-contact. Tears began to prick my eyes and I knew I wouldn't be able to hold it much longer. For some reason, I wanted him to know everything and advise me accordingly.

"Do you study?" he asked. "Yes, sir."

"What does your father do?" "Well, he's a businessman." "And you're here. Why?"

"Just to be self-sufficient, sir," I replied.

"Look, I'm a Supreme Court advocate, and have been practicing for nearly 32 years."

"Oh, that's great, sir!" "And I'm a civil lawyer."

I felt frightened as if he had a criminal chargesheet against me.

"Tell me what the matter is," he asked authoritatively. "Sir…actually…" I fumbled.

"Beta, don't be scared at all. Tell me. Maybe I can be of help," he encouraged.

"I'm really pissed off, sir! My father is never satisfied with whatever I intend to do. Neither can I join his business, nor does he let me pursue my interest." I unloaded my pile of burden to him. He further asked me about Abbu's profession and age. I narrated to him the entire story of my life, right from my toddler days to running away some days ago, along with all those bitter confrontations at home and outside.

I expected him to say, "You father is so ruthless! He should understand the importance of family." Instead, he remained quiet and kept looking at me. At this point, I hoped that he would give me some money at least, if not help.

Finally, he said, "Beta, this is completely unacceptable. You must return to Delhi immediately. He's your father. Never can a father be biased against his own children. I'm a father of four sons and a daughter myself and it's really a wonderful thing. I wish them the best in their respective lives," he told me, his hand on my shoulder.

"But sir…it's different, quite different!»

"No, it's not. You're a teenager. There'll be a lot of highs and lows in your life. How will you tackle it if you run away like this? Be a man, face it like a pro!" He sidelined my emotions.

"Okay sir, I will."

"In case you need any help, let me know. Keep my visiting card with you," he said. He tucked his shirt properly and moved back to his car. There, his driver opened the door for him, he got in and drove off, leaving only a cloud of dust behind.

"Zaid, what are you doing out there?" Ladi summoned me back to the main counter.

I shared this encounter with Ladi who already knew why I had run away. To him, what mattered the most was his work and business.

"Arrey Gabru, let it be. I know that oldie very well. He's gone crazy, nobody listens to him," he said, grinning.

The day had left me deeply disturbed. The words of Mr. Advocate had taken away my sleep. I wondered if the unrest at home must have died out yet. I used to sleep in the courtyard of the dhaba with three other waiters–Bunty, Azam and Rajat. I had not revealed anything to them, but the secret of my past and what I had done was growing heavy within me, threatening to explode like a bomb at any point. I felt as if there were another bomb ticking in Delhi, that would impact the whole Punjab soon too.

The chorus of dawn was mellifluous, but I'd been under a malignant eye. I left for the market, tense and disturbed. Bunty purchased the vegetables, but I kept dithering. I requested Bunty to take over my shift for that day, saying that I wasn't feeling well. He agreed reluctantly, saying that he would go along as long as Ladi didn't find out. When we returned, I was about to go rest when the phone at the reception rang loudly. Bunty picked up the dirty worn-out receiver, while I went into the courtyard.

"There's a call for you from Dilli," Bunty called after me. I was stunned. "He says he's your cousin Abdul."

I couldn't guess who it was since I had cousins by that name on both sides of the family. Besides, what business could either of them have from me? I hadn't told anyone of my location either.

I held the receiver anxiously to my ear.

"How's it going, brother?" a known voice penetrated into my ears. "Oh, asshole..." he started and I immediately recognized my friend.

"Oh, Abdul! How did you get this telephone number?" I asked, puzzled.

"Bro, we're friends and it's the magic of our true friendship," he replied, amused. "Tell me, what happened at home? Why did you skedaddle?" he questioned. I thought of banging the phone right down, but the nostalgia of our closely shared friendship, the cricket matches and juvenile crushes, prevented me from doing it.

"Yaar, it's a long story. The water had passed over my head."

"Are you a coward?" Hehe dared me now.

"No, I'm not. And for God's sake, please don't break me anymore. I'm already annihilated," I pleaded. He stopped and asked me to meet. I didn't appreciate this question. I actually felt ashamed of what I had done.

"Yaar, I'm very near to where you are. Can you meet me?" Abdul revealed in a triumphant voice.

"You can't be where I am, can you?" I prodded further.

"My bro, I've come to Ludhiana for you," Abdul stated gleefully. I felt very skeptical of how he had come to know of my location, but finally agreed on meeting him at Masjid Qudsiya in the city the same day.

It took me around forty minutes to reach the place. I felt both excited and anxious. Each passing moment filled me up with uneasiness, devastation and homesickness. Abdul was a familiar face from home and my heart couldn't put off meeting him. There he was, wandering around the porch of the masjid, two hundred meters away from me. There was nobody else with him. He went over to a betel seller and lit a cigarette at his stall. I remembered how we used to smoke together in school days, albeit amateurishly. My feet felt numb.

"Bismillah (in the name of Allah)," I pronounced and headed towards him.

"Abdul, how are you?" I patted his shoulder from behind. He was exuberant.

He told me how everyone was gravely worried about me at home. The news of my absence had spread like a wildfire to every corner of my locality. After hearing that, I was determined not to return home.

"Will you have something?" Abdul asked, pointing to a tea vendor at the corner of the road.

"Yaar, I should offer you instead. It's Ludhiana and you're my guest," I offered.

"Bro, let's go back. Your *Ammi* has fallen sick and can't eat anything," Abdul recounted grievously. I sighed, but maintained my silence.

"I'm not going back, Abdul. You don't know *Abbu*. He's cruel and fussy about every tiny action I take. He's unhappy with me. What's the point?" I said.

"It's not like that at all, Zaid. Let's go, yaar," he insisted.

"No, I can't," I resisted.

A white Maruti 800 was standing right behind him. Its number plate rang a bell in my mind. To my horror, I saw Rizwan uncle getting out the very next moment. He slammed the driver's door shut.

"Abdul, you betrayed me! Asshole," I abused. He held me tight until Rizwan uncle came to me. I couldn't protest as they took me into the car and back to Delhi. I couldn't utter a word, though I kept wondering what had been my Achilles heel and grimaced.

The Revelation

"What made you run away?" *Ammi* yelled at me.

I stayed quite, looking down on the marble floor of our courtyard. Abbu was not home yet.

"What happened to you, Zaid? Why this?" pleaded *Ammi*.

My heart raced with emotion. The scars on my psyche left by Abbu had hardly faded away, yet there was now a fresh tint on my image.

"I don't know," I uttered, keeping my eyes low. I did not want others seeing me in this situation, particularly our relatives. *Ammi* went into the kitchen, perhaps to bring me some food. It gave me some time to normalize and deliberate. I went over to the washbasin outside the bathroom and looked at myself in the mirror. It reflected my catastrophic condition. I felt ashamed of myself. Surprisingly, I could see specs of grey in my curly hair.

My time in Ludhiana had revealed to me some bitter facts about my life and how the world ran. It had also taught me how dreadful it was to stay away from home. While *Ammi* was still cooking, I rushed into the washroom and took a quick shower. *Ammi* came out with rice and daal, my favourite food, in two big bowls. She knew that I was feeling uncomfortable making eye contact with her, so she went to sit in another room. I wolfed down on the food, wanting more. *Ammi* appeared and refilled the bowls, without asking anything.

To add insult to my injury, *Ammi* had phoned all my students and had told them to resume their studies. I couldn't even request *Ammi* to put it off for the next day. As time went by, my heart palpitated with an even greater intensity. The students came and greeted me; a few of them even touched my feet. It was quite embarrassing. If only they knew what I had done. They told me that I had sparked an interest in them for studying, which had kept them enthusiastic and ambitious, even in my absence.

They held immense regard for me because of my transition from Madarsa to modern education. I was never impressed with these superficial accolades which had no bearing in the world outside Azad Market, which was way advanced and accomplished than the orbit I had been building my castles in. I used to cram one chapter from Rapidex English Book each day and teach it to the students. Surprisingly, they were in awe! I never got any difficult questions from them, and I rode high and easy. Yet, I was always afraid to come across a bright student who could drilled me down. While I was conscience stricken, my students annoyed me even more with their incessant questions of where I had been, who would take care of them in case it occurred again, and how long it would take them to learn English. I had the answer to none.

I realized that only *Ammi* was on speaking terms with me, since my cousins and siblings were upset that I had brought shame to the family. They behaved quite formally with me. We ate together, but our eyes never met. It stung me deeply. When I expressed the same to *Ammi*, she was nonplussed. "Why did you not bring it to my notice earlier?" she asked and I shrugged.

She looked around to make sure that none from our neighborhood was peeping over the high walls of our verandah to gather gossip. Nazia was making her way to the washroom when *Ammi* rebuked her, "Nazia, what's this disgrace? Why won't you talk to your brother? Mend your ways, or else it will be the worst for you." Nazia darted back to her room quietly. "Zaid, let me know if it happens again. I will sort them out," *Ammi* said.

Only Abbu was left now, and not even *Ammi* could talk to him.

It had been hiding from him for five days now. One day, while having a delicious lunch of Parantha and Dahi, *Ammi* said to me, "Try to increase the number of students at your coaching. Tell your existing students to publicise you," *Ammi* suggested. I nodded solemnly, gorging on the food.

Ammi had invited a lady home around 4 PM. It was done in consultation with Mrs. Ajmal, our neighbour, who maintained good contacts with all the divorcees, match-makers and gossipers in the community. At this age, I was damn sure that her visit wouldn't imply a match for me. Since the drawing room was full of my students, the lady sat in one of the bedroom, **Mrs. Ajmal** accompanying her. I peeked though the curtain of my room to see what was happening. *Ammi* went into the kitchen to serve them water.

I returned to my students and their lesson, but they insisted to be let free early that day. After much convincing, I agreed and let them go. While I was washing my face in the basin, the door of the bedroom reflected in the mirror. My heart raced to hear their words, but a little voice inside me instructed me to man up and not indulge in petty gossip. Yet, I had

nothing else to do at home, and the world outside had ostracised me. I finally went to stand by the wall and strained to hear them.

"Afsana, what's the remedy now? " *Ammi* asked the lady.

"Dear sister, your husband's done all this. Rarely have I seen such a case in my career of thirty-two years," the lady replied.

"This is unbelievable!" said Mrs. Ajmal in a rustic tone. My head began to spin with possible explanations. *What had Abbu done now?*

"You should read the last two passages of the Holy Quran twenty-one times, and Zaid will feel better," Ms. Afsana suggested to *Ammi*. I began to sweat.

"Afsana, it happened a year ago as well. Zaid was not behaving well. He used to speak so rudely, but he's a good child of mine. I suspect there's something black at the bottom of this," said *Ammi*, emotional but serious.

"Look, he's been under black-magic for about a decade. It's high time to cure him. Else, he will turn insane," Ms. Afsana added.

"You're right!" said *Ammi* emphatically.

"Does he have evil dreams?" Mrs. Ajmal asked *Ammi*.

"No, he's never shared it with me," said *Ammi*.

"But do perform what I told you to. Inshallah, he will be better. Okay? I should leave now," Ms. Afsana said, standing up.

"Are you sure that his Abbu has caused all this?" asked *Ammi*.

"Yes."

"How can a father do this to his son? It's beyond all possibilities," *Ammi* cried.

"That I can't comment on. But it's your husband's name in my Jinni's record," Ms. Afsana said. I couldn't believe what I was hearing.

At the end, Mrs. Ajmal asked, "What's the name of your Jinni?"

"Khalid is his name. But don't disclose it to anybody, nor pronounce this name ever. **Jinnis** hate to be called by human beings," said Mrs. Afsana and left.

Later, I learnt that Mrs. Afsana had been a renowned predictor since 1982. None of my clan members believed in black magic, sorcery, witchcraft or evil eyes. Such concepts did exist in the Holy Quran, yet no one ever gave it a serious thought, not overtly at least.

I couldn't fathom, however, how *Abbu* could be involved in it.

A Permanent Job

A month had passed, but *Ammi* could no longer relax. All the wrongdoings and incidents refused to dislodge from her brain. I could hardly stand the tension for her, however, I was no mighty force against it. At that point of time, the most prominent victim was me and the enemy was Abbu. Still, *Ammi* never expressed anger towards him. She respected Abbu tremendously, despite knowing of his involvement in such a heinous act.

I believed, she wanted to let it pass. All of us siblings were growing at a rapid rate, and I was getting more attention than ever for my build and appearance increasingly seeming like Abbu. His clothes, shoes and skull cap fitted me well.

Ammi looked particularly radiant at my growth. Her son was turning into a man. Her advice for me to lay low for a few days had worked well for me. I wanted to help her and ease her troubles, yet could do nothing besides helping her wash clothes and hand her my earnings from the coaching. It was not sufficient. One day, while she was pouring out some yummy Kadhi Pakoda into our lunch bowls, I asked her, "Are you all right, *Ammi*?" I feared that she had no one to confide in. All my siblings turned to look at me. While they, particularly Saif and Shazia, pretended to be seriously involved in matter of the family, they did not intend to do so.

"There is nothing as such," said *Ammi*. Until now, she had been under an impression that I was unaware of her discussion with Ms. Afsana, the seer. Since that day, a tinge of animosity had started to creep in my heart towards Abbu. I couldn't help it. The more I strived to stay immune, the more that revelation spun my head. Abbu was still avoiding a confrontation with me. He only came into the house to eat and sleep. Of course, *Ammi* offered him food and took care of all his needs in a timely manner, as usual.

After dinner, *Ammi* sat down in the drawing room to read the Holy Quran. It was unusual to see her do it at this hour, as she always read it right after Fajr (dawn prayer). She looked deep in a spiritual connection, so I didn't intervene. At about 11 PM, while *Ammi* was rinsing utensils in the kitchen, I asked her "You had a long reading of the Holy Quran today. Is everything okay?"

"Yes, alhamdulillah," *Ammi* replied instantly. I wished for *Ammi* to share what truly went on in her mind, why she had done this reading for. Her devotion was never easily understood by me, she had no expectations from this world. The almighty Allah seemed to have smoothened her ways throughout. I waited for her to say further, but she didn't. After she had put all the utensils on the slab, she asked me, "Are you content with your earnings from the coaching?"

I mumbled inaudibly in response.

"Do you know how tough it is to survive on this income? How will you survive after some years? What will you tell the match-makers, that you coach a bunch of students for a living?"

I had no clue what she actually meant. I felt content with my students who respected me and paid me on time.

"You must think of a more permanent job in the market. There're many banks and call-centers around. You will sit in air-conditioned rooms and life will be good."

I nodded. I knew that I was soon to be knocked off my comfort zone.

"Also, don't depend on your father. He has his own destiny and you will have yours," she added. She switched off the courtyard lights, indicating that it was time to sleep, but I wanted to discuss Ms. Afsana's secrets in detail. My vulnerable heart anyway carried innumerable secrets, and the baggage of torments and affliction.

Abbu did not come home even by midnight. We figured that he would be at his brothers' place. We always prayed to God for him to not be at uncle Rizwan's house, for it gave my grandmother–Zubaida Begum, a reason to taunt us each time with her painfully sharp tongue. She was no less than devil incarnate. Her sons were a matter of huge pride for her. She hailed from the same village as *Ammi*. She carried a snooty behavior as she had successfully gotten her six sons and one daughter married. She was living the best life, as the seven wives of her six sons were at her beck and call at all times. My uncle Md. Luqman had been married twice because of her. Both his wives, Shahjahan Begum and Rukhsana Begum lived with him. The latter was twenty-five years younger than her husband. It always baffled me to think about.

Ammi had once narrated to us the whole story of Luqman uncle's bigamous life. It was Daadi who had provoked uncle to get married again when Shahjahan aunty did not bear any children even after many years of their marriage. To my uncle's credit, his personality stunned even his nephews. He hugely resembled Jackie Shroff–the popular Bollywood actor. He'd happily been living with Shahjahan Aunty for many years, and did not desire to get married again, but Daadi had ceaselessly egged him on for it. Finally, it happened without any restraint.

These two uncles, Md. Rizwan and Md. Luqman, lived in a double-storied house across Nawab Ganj, while the rest of my uncles lived in Seelampur, Delhi. The ground floor of the building had a glass godown which always clinked like a bar. Daadi lived on the first floor of this house along with Daada–Haji Md. Usman, a man of unshakable faith in the almighty Allah. He was about eighty years of age and I called him Abba. Abba hardly intervened in any of his sons' lives. Despite being a grandfather to twenty-two grandchildren,

Abba mostly maintained his silence. Daadi and Abba shared an abiding bond between them.

Whenever Abba came back from Fakhruddin Masjid– the biggest mosque in the vicinity, Daadi always had a betel leaf ready for him. He would frown if his *paan* was not ready for him upon his return. Abba vividly remembered the partition of 1947, and often narrated painful stories from that time. He always wore a pair of loose pyjamas and a kurta–the Islamic attire, had a short grey beard, to which he fortnightly applied Mehndi (myrtle). It rendered a shining touch to his beard. Owing to his calm nature, Daadi had dominated the house since they had gotten married. The diktat was always from her, and nobody could overturn it.

Fondly, Abbu never missed a visit to this house. Even with the tightest schedule, he always managed to go there at least once a week, mostly on Saturday nights, and participated in trivial discussions with his family members, while my aunts remained on kitchen duty the whole night. I had often been the topic of their late-night talks. It was one such night for him. We all retired to our beds unassumingly.

The next morning, as *Ammi* was preparing breakfast, I asked her if something was bothering her. She snapped at me and told me to mind my own business, and hunt for a more permanent employment. "Why don't you go for interviews like Adil, our neighbour?" *Ammi* asked, sounding frustrated, almost angry.

She got Parantha and Dahi for me, yet I didn't quite feel an appetite. She pushed aside the curtains of the room angrily, and I feared for their longevity. "Where shall I try my luck, *Ammi*?"

"Why don't you go speak to Adil? He will certainly guide you through."

Never in a hundred years could that be possible. Adil was devastatingly studious, but self-centred and selfish. I didn't want to be a subject of his humiliation. "I won't approach him. He's mean, too mean!" I argued.

"Don't worry, I can speak to Nooran bhabi, his mother. You have to play smart to get things going," *Ammi* smiled.

Abbu was still not speaking to me, though I often found him talking to and laughing with Nazia and Saif.

"*Ammi,* please say dua (prayer) for me. I will go for an interview tomorrow, inshallah," I said, rolling a little finger in my left ear. My interest in my coaching was depleting. I earnestly prayed for Allah to send Khalid–the Jinni, to get me a lucrative work option.

"Sure, it's out of question. I always do, beta... May success attend to you!"

The next morning, I woke up from a restless sleep at 9 AM, well before the rest of the house, put on my best clothes and set out to hunt for a job. I took a bus to reach my destination–Kamla Nagar, where I had seen a series of hoardings and promising call-center jobs with a 100% guaranteed employment. Besides, it was the nearest location from my house. The bus dropped me near Hansraj College, Malka Ganj, a few paces away from Kamla Nagar.

Making my way through the fashionable DU students with the latest techno-accessories and swanky cars and skimpy outfits, I reached the Kolhapur road market. The shopkeepers and vendors there had no idea where to lead me, so I asked a college student, "Do you know where the job consultancies are?"

"Yes, there're many. Are you looking for a BPO job?" he asked.

Little did I know what BPO was. I just needed a job. Just then, my gaze landed on a signboard that read, *Pathways Consultants–Come in empty-handed, go with a job in hand.* I thanked the student and rushed towards the building.

"Are you here for an interview?" the receptionist asked in a mellifluous voice.

"Yes, I am," I replied just as sweetly.

"Okay. What company are you here for?" she asked. I didn't have the slightest idea.

"Please sit down. Vaishali ma'am will see you in a bit. Meanwhile, please fill in this form," she said smiling. The form was supposed to be duly filled in with all the academic records. I looked around to see the number of interviewees in the room. It was full of girls and boys, most of them were north-eastern. I filled in my name, father's name, correspondence address and date of birth quite neatly. My fingers trembled at '10th Grade marks obtained' and grudgingly put in 41%.

A girl, perhaps Vaishali, approached me and asked, "Hi, how can I help you?"

"My name is Zaid," I managed to stutter out.

"Can you briefly run me through your profile?" she asked grimly.

"Sorry?" I asked, absolutely confused.

Most of the boys in the room chuckled. "Tell me something about yourself," she simplified.

"Yes ma'am. My name is Md. Zaid, I live in Azad Market. I did my schooling from Shafiq Memorial School, Delhi," I replied, sweating a bit.

"Okay," she sighed disappointedly. "How did you spend yesterday?" She had posed a terrible question for sure.

"Well, I got up at seven, then went for a morning walk. Afterwards, I took breakfast and..."

She stopped me midway. "Sorry, what did you do after the morning walk?"

"Umm...I took breakfast."

"Are you sure that you *took* the breakfast?" She repeated, grinning.

"Yes, I took breakfast."

Everybody gave me a disgusting look. When I expected sympathy, they gave me mockery. How could I have been wrong, I wondered. I had been teaching students English for about two years.

"And what are you wearing?" Vaishali started again.

I looked down to see my black T–shirt captioned in yellow 'Focus on 80s'.

"Please wear formals to interviews, as they have," she said, pointing to the other students. She then walked away to the water dispenser.

"Mr. Zaid, you may leave for the day," the receptionist pronounced in a business-like tone. So capricious she had been, and such an imbecile I was!

A definite dent had been put in my inflated ego from the coaching. *Ammi*'s concern for my job now seemed legitimate. I felt ashamed of what I earned from my coaching. I felt as if I had been committing a cardinal sin.

It was evening by the time I reached home. I knocked on the main door, but it was locked. As was the practice, however, I found the key hidden behind the water meter right next to the gate. I changed into my kurta pyjama and decided to offer my evening ablutions at home since *Ammi* was not around. Saif came in around

7.30 from his tuition classes.

"Where've they gone?" I asked

"I don't know. There were here before I left. Maybe, they have gone to the market to shop," said Saif, drinking water from a pet bottle. I lay down in my bed and dozed off for a nap. The telephone rang after a while, but I yelled at Saif to answer it.

"Bhai, Abbu beat up *Ammi* again. Nazia, Shazia and *Ammi* are at Daadi's house," he blurted, fuming, after hanging up the call.

"Let's go there," I said.

"Hold on, Shazia just told me on the phone that we should stay here. *Ammi* will deal with it herself."

My anxiety rose up and my blood boiled in my veins. "Saif, when did it occur? You left home at five and Abbu must've been in Mundka then."

He remained silent and ignorant. We waited for further news. I imagined strangulating my Daadi and all the others who were a cause of our misery.

"We must go there, God forbid if something wrong has happened," Saif suggested.

"Hmm, yes," I echoed. As we rushed to the gate, I saw Rizwan uncle and Abbu crossing the road to come to the house. I cursed my luck and retreated back in. The two men did not come to the house though, but headed towards Ram Bagh road (main road leading towards ISBT, Kashmere Gate) instead.

"Where are they coming from?" I asked, gritting my teeth.

"Daadi's house. Where else?" said Saif.

They stopped by the road side, hired an auto and left. It was 9.30 now and *Ammi* and my sisters had not returned yet. We marched swiftly to Nawab Ganj now. It was completely deserted. We reached the house and climbed up the stairs to find *Ammi* and my sisters just leaving. *Ammi*'s face had turned pale and colorless like I had never seen before. My sisters were quiet, but had clouds of anger and indignation around them.

"I will destroy you," Saif shouted at the top of his voice. I escorted *Ammi* and my sisters down.

"Saif, come down immediately," roared *Ammi*.

"I can't come. It's the daily drama now. We'll have to end it," said Saif, still at the door. It definitely increased the tension all around. I was more worried about the consequences; particularly, Abbu's barbarism. I pulled Saif down, all the way to the street. I felt terribly helpless and small.

We got back home somehow. Saif pulled out two cold water bottles from the fridge. *Ammi* and my sisters gulped down the water as if they had been thirsty for ages.

"What happened? How did it start?" I asked, looking into their eyes. My sisters waited for *Ammi* to speak.

"The old story again, I don't cook as well as your aunties," said *Ammi*, tears rolling down her cheeks. Nazia offered her a handkerchief to wipe her face, but *Ammi* ignored it. She'd abysmally been wounded this time.

"But Abbu must've been in Mundka from 10 am onwards," Saif asked, looking at his sisters.

"No, he came home around 4 for lunch, Aloo Gosht," explained Shazia.

"Did he not like the Aloo Gosht?" asked Saif, nonplussed. *Ammi* simply nodded. After so many years of their marriage, it sounded off.

"What shall we do now? It's too much! He's never been so ruthless," said Saif and our sisters agreed.

"You're not going to do anything. He's your father and you always have to respect and revere him," said *Ammi*, still deep in her emotions.

"But we must at least escalate it to Naani," Nazia suggested. The rest of us agreed, even though we knew that she would never agree to it. It was below her principles.

Whack! *Ammi* slapped Saif and Shazia. "Don't you dare speak to anyone about it.," she added further. We resigned to our fate.

An End and a Beginning

"Sir, we won't be able to continue these classes," said Azam, one of my students at home.

I had realized recently what my teaching was worth, but this one seemed determined to extirpate my humble image that I had formed with so much difficulty over the last two years.

"Okay, but is there a particular reason for it?" I asked, feigning nobility. They all looked at one another, as if I had never been their tutor. No student had left willingly before.

"Sir, you remain absent more than often. It hugely hampers our studies. My parents would like me to switch," said Azam, grimly. "We never get an intimation in case of an off. Most days, we sit for hours in this room before going back home without any lesson," added Mohsin. I wished to disappear from the class. "My parents are pressurising me to join another coaching in the locality," said Sana. One by one, they all put forth their reasons and I let them go. I couldn't even retain a single student, and they were all gone.

My safe haven had been destroyed. I feared that I wouldn't be able to realize my *Ammi*'s dream of seeing me earn more. I remained poring over my English book to maintain the pretence for *Ammi*'s sake. She was washing clothes in the courtyard, after which she went up to the terrace to put them out to dry. Finally at 6 PM, I berthed the book back on the table along with two other books.

The sight of the empty room made me feel crippled. I longed for the same students I had loathed until an hour ago. *Ammi* had once said, "It's not about your willingness to work, rather you must have something to work on." I came to realize her words now.

Abbu knocked on the door and came in. It wasn't the right time to discern what Abbu had done the other day and how he should be held further responsible. I had my own failures to lament upon. Things were lumbering down, while *Ammi* needed me to skyrocket. *Ammi* was always quick to recover from the anguish that Abbu caused.

The landline rang just then. Nazia answered. It was a call from Ms. Afsana who demanded to speak to *Ammi*. "*Ammi*, there's a call for you," Nazia gave out a shout. Abbu was in the washroom. He used to change into a dhoti and kurta at night. I heard Salam being exchanged between *Ammi* and Ms. Afsana. The conversation went on for the next fifteen minutes. Ms. Afsana supplemented that Abbu had fatally conspired an occult act against me. The spell had been making a difference since my infancy, as per her astrological findings. *Ammi* just nodded and replied in a Yes or no, for the fear of Abbu hearing her. The reason behind Ms. Afsana's proactive gesture was to fetch some fee, which *Ammi* had forgotten to pay the last interaction.

"Okay, please visit again. Allah hafiz!" said *Ammi* and hung up.

"Who's call was that?" Abbu enquired, suspecting her. We never received a phone call after 9.

"It was Aapa's (my Naani) call," *Ammi* replied, fluffing the mattress.

The next day, Abbu passionately acted upon his life-principles and dismantled the landline. He simply held the box without the wires and asked for a bag to carry it in as he left. Later in Mundka, he talked to some fellow traders who helped him get to a telephone exchange, where he extracted information about the the last call received by greasing the palms of the officers there. It turned out to be Mohd. Salem–Ms. Afsana's husband.

Abbu immediately dialed and talked with Ms. Afsana, and snubbed her for carrying out resolutions to evil magic. As far as I knew, however, she was unruffled by such a disgrace. She genuinely knew how to cure an occult-stricken patient. Thereby, she had been massively successful for nearly two decades. To Abbu's acute consternation, she said before hanging up, "Do you think that all your abominable deeds are hidden? I'm profusely aware of what all you've hatched for your wife and son, and what further damages you're determined to take on. Mr. Farooq, fear the almighty Allah! You're ruining your family for the sake of a divorcee who's nineteen years younger than you. She deserted her first husband. Don't go for such a marriage. It's all lust! Fear the Almighty."

Abbu grew short of breath with anxiety and his vision blurred. He wrapped everything up quickly to return home. Gopal found his hastiness and twitchiness quite odd. When he asked his employer about the same, he dismissed Gopal with a stern word. His confidante Rashid had not come to work that day either. He left Mundka at 3:20 PM. While *Ammi* and the siblings were horrified back home by the absence of the telephone, Abbu was bitterly jolted by Ms. Afsana words.

In the absence of my students, I had little to do besides doing some household chores and engaging with my siblings or books. I read for most part of the day to give *Ammi* the impression that I was doing something constructive. I thought of telling her that I was preparing for a job interview, but hesitated.

At 4 PM, I left for Kamla Nagar again, wearing the same black T-shirt. I couldn't afford new clothes yet. The thought of going into another BPO office terrified me, as I still felt quite ashamed of my previous experience here. My gaze suddenly fell upon a flex hoarding that read, *G-Tec Computer education (Govt. Approved)*. Computers had always been my Achilles' heels. My classes at school had not given me any practical skill in working with a computer, so I decided to give it a try.

As I read through the courses offered in Tally, accounting, Java and C++, my mind took me back to the memory of my great-grandmother Bismillah Begum who would fondly call me 'Fauji' since she desired me to join the Indian Army. She had passed away when I was only seven. I wondered if that would be a better calling for me, but then shook my head to dismiss the thought. What caught my attention just then was 'Free Spoken English classes on Saturdays' written at the bottom. I decided to enquire about it.

The place looked less than appropriate for an educational hub. It's front windows were broken, the staircase reeked of mould and damp, the walls were dirty and there was barely enough light inside. I heaved a sigh of impatience, thinking of my great- grandmother's words again and climbed up the metaphorical dark tunnel, hoping for light at the end.

A beautiful receptionist in a red silk top greeted me with a, "Good evening, sir! How may I help you?" The name tag on one side of her chest read Akanksha Mathur.

"I want to know about the free spoken English classes," I said.

"There's no free class. We offer that additional class to our existing students on Saturdays," she said. "Gaurav sir, a person here wants to enquire about the English class," she said, knocking on the cabin wall behind her. I felt slightly more confident now since she had well understood my pedestrian English. It was a milestone, in a way. Gaurav gestured me in.

"Hi, I'm Gaurav. How're you doing?" he asked smiling.

"I'm very well, thank you," I replied, looking through the cabin at Akanksha.

Gaurav looked at the caption of my T- shirt and we exchanged a warm smile.

"We offer English classes on Saturdays..." he started. "Yes, I know," I interrupted him. My confidence boosted even more since he had started talking in

Hindi.

"What do you do?" Gaurav asked.

"Well, I teach English," I said, confident and smiling. "Where do you teach?" he asked in a curious manner. "I've been teaching at several institutions for about

three years," I replied.

"I need an English trainer here for the Saturday classes. Can you make it?"

"Umm, Saturday. What shall be the duration of the classes?"

"There're two batches–two hours each," he said, taking a sip of water.

"Yes, I can," I consented, smiling.

"What's your expectation?" he asked, holding a notebook now. I feared he would see through my lie any moment now, but I went on with my pretence.

"How much do you pay?" I asked. "Five hundred," he said.

"Let's make it seven, since there're two batches to look after," I proposed. I couldn't believe my own audacity.

"That's too much. Let's make Rs. 650/- to start with," he concluded. I instantly agreed.

It had all been a verbal agreement, with no written documented proof, but I didn't care. I treated myself to a Dahi Bhalla in the market outside and rushed home to tell *Ammi* everything. I hired an auto to Azad Market instead of hustling on a bus. I basked in the glory of this little success and the world seemed beautiful.

I wondered how pleased everyone would be back home to hear of my success. My auto ran out of fuel at a red light a kilometre away from my house, so I paid him and decided to travel the remaining distance on foot. I felt unbeatable, ecstatic and impatient to get home. I danced and sang *Everybody* by Backstreet Boys, which was in fact the only English song I knew, albeit partially.

"Who's there?" Nazia responded as I knocked on the front door. She came to open it, then turned around and rushed back before I had even entered. She pulled off a white dupatta from an iron rod placed in the middle of the courtyard and covered her head with it, anticipating Abbu coming back. *Ammi* was nowhere to be seen. I checked the kitchen and the storeroom for her, but she wasn't around.

"Is everything okay? Where's *Ammi*?" I asked Nazia. I had a sinking feeling inside that something terrible had happened.

"As long as Abbu is around, he would never let us get over this trauma," said Nazia, frustrated. Her eyes swam with tears.

"*Ammi, Ammi*!" I shouted frantically.

"She's on the terrace," Nazia revealed, pointing up. I ran upstairs incautiously. *Ammi* was letting out laundry to dry.

"*Ammi*, what happened now?" I asked, holding her divine hand.

"Nothing, where did you go?" she asked. There wasn't a hint of grief on her face. I lumbered back slowly and my mind fuzzed over. The G-Tec news was too small a triumph to compete with the misery of this household.

"Tell me, what happened?" I insisted.

"Arrey, nothing. Your Abbu came back early to meet a client, and had lunch here," she unfurled a piece of cloth, smiling.

"And insulted your cooking again, right?" I questioned, gritting my teeth.

"That's fine!" she said, pretending to be busy.

"He's the most relentlessly bad father on this planet, I'm telling you," I simmered.

Ammi looked back and said, "Curse him all you want, but you will never ever enter heaven. A father is the door to the Almighty's kingdom."

"You're speaking in favor of a father who's always harbored a desire to kill you and me," I said, looking down into the courtyard. I didn't care if Abbu heard me, he had made our lives so immeasurably miserable that I was ready to drop down to any devil's knees to alleviate the suffering. "What're you made of, *Ammi*? He's not the author of our fate," I said, almost going insane. "You prayed, cared and pulled him out of a fatal illness, and are unaffected by whatever atrocities he does upon us. It's extreme!" I spat.

"Shut up! Don't you dare talk that way," she said, preparing her right hand to slap me.

I was in no mood to give in though, neither could I keep the venom inside. "He's been conspiring to kill you first and then me, did you know? Afterwards, he shall remarry," I revealed.

"What? Marriage?" *Ammi* asked. Both of us were aware of his bigamous plans, but her heart was an ocean.

"Thanks to Mundka and the people there who blurted out bits of information to me," I said in a high- pitched voice.

The sound of the evening Azaan filled the air, and we fell quiet. I mumbled quietly along.

"Go offer Namaz. You mustn't miss it," *Ammi* said, intending to evade the issue at hand as usual. I stomped over to the mosque half-heartedly.

Nazia later narrated to me what Abbu had done earlier that day. He questioned *Ammi* how she dared to contact Ms. Afsana. He vehemently mentioned that if someone had a suspicion on him, they should ask him directly, and not seek external knowledge on his character. He had said it all after plonking over a plate of chicken-korma on the bed. He then yanked *Ammi*'s hand and pushed her over to the wall mercilessly. Nazia kept standing at the door helplessly. The ghastly drama went on till *Ammi* ran out and hid herself in another room, bolting the door from the inside.

I didn't want to meet Abbu's eyes anymore, and thankfully, he didn't pass by me. At about 11 PM, *Ammi* asked us where Abbu was. We didn't know. "He must be sipping tea made by Shama Aunty. Huh, bitch!" I said. *Ammi* stared at me but remained quiet. Perhaps she had given up silencing me. She picked up her Tasbeeh (beaded garland) and started meditating as she always did before going to sleep. Perhaps she thought that I was trying to break her and Abbu up, when all I wanted was the opposite–peace at home. It was for that reason that I had started going to Mundka with Abbu. I decided to reverse the situation, all the while wondering why *Ammi* wouldn't question Abbu about his rumoured affair.

Day One at G-Tec

"Who's gonna bore us today?" asked a male student sitting in the first row of the classroom.

„Damn, we've never had a nice trainer who is hot and a hunk," another girl echoed her friend's words.

"We want a young dashing teacher," said another.

Shockingly, it was all happening right in front of me. I had reached the class early and waited for all the students to arrive. The furniture in the class as rackety and dusty, apparently unmaintained for decades. The room was big enough to accommodate about twenty- five people, but only about eleven had showed up by 9:30. I was keen to see how they'd respond to my teaching. An office boy knocked and came in with an attendance register.

Unassumingly, I had taken a seat amongst the other students, but now my secret was out as the office boy spotted me, handed me the register and said, "Sir, Gaurav sir has sent this for you. Please mark the attendance of both the batches." His eyes traversed to the girls sitting in the room, but as I stood up, he rushed out of the class. All the students turned around to look at me with their eyes wide open.

They mumbled their apologies and greeted me with a smile so warm and regardful that I forgot all that they had said just a while ago. They listened attentively as I started my lecture on 'Letters in English' and parts of speech. The clock struck 12 PM, indicating the start of the second lecture

"Alright, let's call it a day!" I announced, and the student filed out of the class one after the other. The commenters from before gave me a solemn look, but I laughed it off in a pretentious tone. *Ammi*'s teachings had ingrained in me not to retaliate.

The second batch was awaiting my arrival in another classroom. My heart thumped harder to see the exceeding number of girls in this batch. However, I had gained much confidence after my first lecture. I recollected that Gaurav had told me that the institute predominantly attracts a govt. school crowd, and it was apparent by their rough appearance and hesitant demeanour.

"Are we settled down?" I asked, but nobody responded. I repeated myself, but there was no response still. I got frustrated and asked, "Shall we start the class?"

"Yes, sir," came a girl's melodious voice from the back. I looked up in surprise.

"Hello sir, what's your name?" she asked, meeting my eyes. The first thing I noticed were her beautiful earrings, then her deep brownish eyes, and then her beautiful face. She was impeccably dressed in a black top and light blue jeans.

"Well, I'm...I was saying..." I stuttered nervously under her unwavering gaze. I had to remind myself to breathe.

"Sir, you didn't tell us your name," she asked again, shuffling in her chair.

"I'm Md. Zaid," I said, clearing my throat.

My gaze rested on the knuckles of her soft and slender fingers, then traversed to her silver painted nails.

"You're going to learn a score of things today," I started, but was interrupted by her again as she said,

«Sir, let's just have a round of introductions today."

I had been wanting to know her name, so I agreed to a brief round of introductions. She was the one to go first. "Hi everyone, I'm Sneha Kaushik from Kamla Nagar, Delhi."

Everyone applauded her, much to my own pleasure. I wanted nothing more than to keep listening to her talk and be under her benumbing spell. Her gaze induced me to swim in my adolescent dreams. Perhaps the students realized that their new gullible trainer was nothing but a recipe for disaster for them.

"Let's learn how to introduce ourselves more impressively," I announced, and the students nodded affirmatively. "What do you do?" I probed further.

"I'm pursuing B.A. from DU," she replied confidently. I flushed, thinking that she would perhaps know my subject better than me. "My father is a Supreme Court Judge and *Ammi* is a homemaker," she added. The word 'Judge' sent a shiver down my spine.

At the end of that class, she left with a sweet goodbye to me. Everything about her, from her countenance, to her hair and her delicate slender fingers felt like drops of water over my parched heart. I went back home, smiling at the image of her in my mind. At 11 PM that night, I told *Ammi* about this new gig I had landed. She beamed with happiness, but my excitement was rooted elsewhere. The thought of Sneha's father did terrify me though.

Finally, I decided to take *Ammi*'s opinion on it. "*Ammi*, should we ever befriend lawyers?" I asked her.

"Never. They're very dangerous people. May Allah always keep us away from the police, lawyers and doctors!" said *Ammi*, growing tense.

"Yes, that's what I've heard," Nazia echoed *Ammi*'s sentiments. My pulse quickened. I could've ignored Nazia, but not *Ammi*. Everybody went to bed at 11.45, but I kept thinking about Sneha, missing her countenance, her hair, and her nail-paint.

Since I wasn't to see Sneha until next Saturday, *Ammi*'s words suppressed all my desires to be with. Furthermore, *Ammi* told me to be cautious at every step of life. "Zaid, you're the face of our family. I trust you the most," she said, tousling my curly hair. I tried to suppress my feelings for

Sneha, but everything around me led to the thoughts of her alone. All conversations led to my classes and students. Unable to keep her image away from my mind, I even tried dabbling in romantic poetry. It was never my cup of tea, nor had I felt this way before. I did not think I would ever be besotted with a girl. Her hypnotic eyes persistently haunted me. I scribbled:

Those Blissful Eyes

I'm in those blissful eyes,

I long for those meaningful eyes, Certainly, their move moves me They leave an imprint on me.

I drown in their intensity as, The night shuts in a dark city

They're celestial light, ambrosia and utopia The allies seem wider now; there's Gloria! O dear! Please raise your eyes,

For the gust of breeze magnifies

They possess the sounds of dew

Angel! Look here, my desires' few. Never lower your eyes, never

As I might turn insane forever! They convey warmth, ecstasy Don't lock them; my curiosity! I'm in those blissful eyes,

I long for those meaningful eyes.

I dodged every unpleasant encounter at home, while also fearing that Sneha's chapter could beget even more shambles. My memory of my first crush, my primary school teacher, had now faded away, but this apparent infatuation continuously suffered the threat of both our fathers.

Ammi's words pulled me out of my reverie. "Is there someone at the door?" she asked.

"Yes, I will check," I said, rubbing my temples.

It was Rizwan uncle. "Salam," I offered my greetings. "Walaikumasslam," he responded with a deathly gaze. It was unexpected of him to drop in all alone.

Ammi and my siblings were in the other room, engrossed in chit-chat. "Can I get a glass of water, please?" he demanded tauntingly. We expected that his visit wasn't going to be short lasting. Rizwan uncle had been nice to us in the past, bringing us fruits and taking us all out with his own family, since Abbu never did. He even cracked jokes with us and condemned Abbu for his bad habits, temperament and approach. However, a changed man had come to visit us today. *Ammi* and the siblings, however, were still under the old impression of him. Since he was fond of mutton and eggs cooked by *Ammi,* she scurried over to the kitchen to fix some boiled eggs for him.

"Tell your *Ammi* not to get involved in such formalities. I've already had dinner," uncle said to Nazia. It was probably the first indirect dialogue by him for *Ammi*. He then asked for a toothpick and began nibbling through his sharp pale teeth.

"How's Shama? Is everyone all right at home?" *Ammi* asked, smiling.

After a long gaze, uncle shrugged and said, "I don't know." He had never been so unfriendly with us. "You shouldn't be asking about my family," he added testily.

Ammi's smile disappeared. Saif and I exchanged wary looks. He placed himself precariously on the edge of the bed, as if he would stand up and leave any moment. Everyone at home turned their attention towards him. Nazia stood up to get water for him, but Saif elbowed her not to. This was enough to trigger him.

"What's this drama you've created? Don't you feel ashamed?" he asked, directly facing *Ammi*. We looked on quietly.

"What do you mean?" *Ammi* asked anxiously.

"As if you don't know," he jeered ruthlessly. He lit a cigarette right there inside the room. *Ammi* didn't dare to stop him. After all, he was the apple of Abbu's eyes.

"Why don't you help solve it?" he asked, turning towards me.

"Ummm, me?" I said, baffled.

"Yes, you," he said frowning. *Ammi* looked impatient to bury the discussion. All of us siblings now looked at uncle Rizwan for a revelation.

"Don't drag my kids into it. I'll answer all your questions," *Ammi* breathed.

"What do you want? Why've you created this drama, that too after all these years of your marriage?" he spewed out hot words. The room plunged into darkness. *Ammi* tried to clarify each altercation, but in vain. "What to do now? Farooq bhai is not in a good state of mind. He's quite disturbed," uncle said, coughing. I handed him a spittoon.

"We've never bothered him for anything, I swear on God!" *Ammi* said exasperatedly.

There was a knocking on the door just then. "Goodness me! It must be Abbu," I said, panicking.

"Don't you worry. I'm here," uncle assured us.

I unlocked the door. Abbu wore a tough look, his lips tightly sealed. Abbu came into the room quietly and sat down on the other end of the bed. None of us had the courage to say the first word. We knew Abbu could invest the whole night in that manner, fagging on cigarettes with no result. He loved to indulge in trivialities. On the other hand, *Ammi* seemed like she wanted to bail as early as possible, but Abbu was a revengeful man that night.

"Bhai, what should we do?" uncle Rizwan asked Abbu, rubbing his nose.

"What? It's quite obvious that she doesn't like to get along with me," Abbu accused, tapping his cigarette at the edge of the ashtray. I was stunned to hear such a disgusting response from him. He had turned the situation around to present himself as the victim. All of us looked at *Ammi* to take the charge.

"Bhabi, what's all this happening?" uncle asked calmly. *Ammi*'s eyes filled with tears, and she covered half her face with a dupatta that she usually wore for Namaz.

"Why would I want to spoil this relationship? It has been so many years and we have four grown-up children now. Who wouldn't want to get along in this world in such a situation?" *Ammi* said, beseeching uncle Rizwan to understand. He didn't react. I felt my mind and emotions going numb with each passing second. I anticipated that Abbu wouldn't intervene until uncle gestured him to do so.

Just then, *Ammi* started looking for her slippers, perhaps to leave the room and attend the loo.

Whack! Whack! Whack! Abbu hit *Ammi* in her shoulders. Then, he jerked at *Ammi*'s plait with mighty force. I tried to constrain him, but he had gone completely berserk. Since I had now grown taller than Abbu, I wedged myself between Abbu and *Ammi*. Surprisingly, uncle did nothing but offer a verbal reconciliation. Abbu got tired and sat back down. Tufts of *Ammi*'s torn hair were visible on the floor. *Ammi* sobbed. In fact, all my siblings wept bitterly. Abbu and uncle stood up to go out. Abbu slept peacefully at uncle's home perhaps, while we lay sleepless in our house.

The following day was a Sunday. We expected Abbu to come back home in sometime and have lunch with us, as was the practice. He did come, but only to get his clothes. Since he didn't wish to speak to *Ammi*, he commanded Nazia to bundle up all his clothes and other belongings. I stepped forth to speak to him, but he turned a blind eye. He went over to the washbasin to wash his face. I wished that mirror over it could show the world his real face.

"*Ammi*, he is leaving with his clothes," Nazia whispered.

"Don't let him go. Stop him!" *Ammi* cried, drenched in sweat. Despite his unpardonable brutalities, she held him in high regard. Amidst *Ammi*'s painful wails and cries requesting him to stay, Abbu held the bundle of his belongings over his shoulder and left the house.

Abbu's First Marriage

Gaurav, the director of G-Tech called me up one day.

"How're you doing, sir?" he asked. I had been absent for about a month and a half. *Ammi* had motivated me to continue, but I didn't show up on any of the weekends in between. I remained quiet as *Ammi* was cleaning the room right behind me. I waited for her to leave the room.

"And what're you upto?" I asked.

"Sir, it's been too long. Can you please update me if you're joining us back?" he asked in a sharp tone. I still couldn't utter a word since *Ammi* was still there. "Why don't you speak up?" he stressed. This time, he had omitted the title 'sir'.

Ammi finally reached the doorway and I sighed, but Gaurav had disconnected the call by then. "Damn it," I cursed and banged the receiver down. The phone rang again in a few seconds.

I picked up and explained, "Hi Gaurav, I am awfully sorry for not being able to answer that last time." He pardoned me immediately, and listened empathetically as I narrated to him all that had happened at home in this period of time. Abbu had walked out with all his things to live at my grandmother's house.

"Oh, that's ridiculous. It's terribly sad," he said. "What will happen now?"

"I don't know. There is nobody here with us to take care," I said mournfully.

"You should approach your grandparents," Gaurav suggested and we hung up.

At around five in the evening that day, I knocked on the door of Dadi's house. I hoped that there would be nobody there except my grandparents, but Shama aunty opened the door and let me in. I walked into the courtyard and saw five pairs of footwear lying outside the living room, indicating the number of people sitting inside. I figured I had dropped in at the wrong hour, but it was impossible to back out now.

My glance landed on Abbu and Dadi first. "Asslamualikum," I greeted them all. Abbu and Dadi were sitting beside Dada, while Rizwan uncle was lying in one corner. He got up upon seeing me. Hardly had I taken off my shoes, when Dadi began to shower expletives at me, "Swine! You're at the root of all this."

A look of surprise flashed across Dada's face. "Are you mad or what?" he rebuked Dadi. Rizwan uncle offered me to sit down, and Shama aunty offered me a glass of water which I refused. Abbu cast a wary and disgusted glance at me. I tried to hold his gaze, but he looked away. The sight pained me, but I stayed calm throughout. "Why don't you take your Abbu home?" Dadi asked me, her brows twitching.

I was glad for her words. "Dadi, I'm here to bury the hatchet. Abbu, let's go home," I said. My heart was thumping with anxiety and terror.

"He will not go anywhere, you dog!" Rizwan uncle thundered. I wanted to educate him on who was acting more like a dog, but I let everything go. Abbu remained a calm spectator, immune to the rebukes directed against me.

"Call your *Ammi*. We will talk to her," Shama aunty said, taking charge.

"Is it necessary? I'm here to reconcile on her behalf," I said, feeling vindictive.

Whack! Whack! Whack! Both Abbu and Rizwan uncle hit me square in my nose. It started to bleed. I got scared seeing blood dripping down onto my shirt. Dada didn't say a word as Abbu beat me black and blue right in front of him. He climbed onto my chest and didn't let me breathe.

"Beat this bastard more," encouraged Shama Aunty. " Leave him," Rizwan uncle said.

Their faces got blurred. I wanted to run away, fearing for my life. I struggled to get up and walked out of the room, forgetting to even put my shoes back on. I felt like a puny non-entity in the arena of the mighty. As I was just exiting the courtyard, I heard Dadi say, "Thank God, this swine doesn't know about your first marriage."

I stopped to overhear their conversation. My nose still bled, but not more than my heart. Experiencing blows upon blows, I felt as if Gabriel–the angel of death had transported my soul to an alien planet. *Well done, Abbu!* I said in my heart.

No one noticed me except the nosey neighbourhood shopkeeper, Shamim Bhai. He looked at me standing against a corner of his shop, bleeding and tattered, but did not bother to even step out, let alone help.

I rushed home and hammered on the door frantically. Nazia came to open it, but when she saw me, all colour left her face. "How did this happen? she gasped.

"*Ammi, Ammi*!" I screamed as I entered the house. Nazia told me that she had gone to the market, and brought me a glass of chilled water. She then left to look for some antiseptic ointment for me. *Ammi* returned in half an hour. I had cleaned up my wounds by then. I narrated the entire confrontation to her. *Ammi* and Nazia cursed Dadi and Rizwan uncle, but not Abbu. There were no limits to my frustration. I wondered if either of them knew about Abbu's first marriage. I longed to unfold this enigma.

My nose burned with pain and regret coursed through me. I realised I shouldn't have acted on Gaurav's suggestion. In retrospect, I should've discussed it with *Ammi*. She offered me some tea and a parantha.

"He will never come back," Nazia grunted. Her words stung me as I realized that in Abbu's absence, I would have to shoulder all the minor and major responsibilities around the house. *Ammi* maintained her silence.

Suddenly, there was loud thumping on the door. I asked Nazia to go open it, thinking that if it were Abbu and Rizwan uncle, they wouldn't hit her. Unfortunately, it was Shama aunty who smacked Nazia across her face as she opened the door to her, Abbu, Rizwan uncle and a couple more young men behind them. I rushed to silence the nonsense.

"Beat them! Turn them out of my house," Abbu said in a stentorian tone.

"Allah, please help," *Ammi* mumbled, looking up. "Stop them! Someone," Nazia yelled.

The door of our neighbors squeaked open and the old and wrinkled Mrs. Ajmal stepped out. Everyone was stunned to see her standing in our defence. Nazia was sobbing, while *Ammi* was stroking her head to calm her down. Allah had heard *Ammi*'s prayers, for the angry mob left the place.

My Abbu's brothers had been extremely pally with me for as long as I could remember, but they were all slowly being turned against us. Saif had seen them all getting together at Dadi's place. I changed my mosque to go for prayer, so they didn't see me. Yet, things were not in my favour. Tahir Chaudhry, my eldest uncle's son spotted me when I went to offer my evening prayers at a distant mosque. He was a merciless giant–6'2 in height with 120 kgs heavy, and had a reputation for beating people up. Before this matter, he had often appreciated me for my English-speaking skills, but I was interested to know how he would react now. However, he conveniently ignored me, moving aside to lace up his shoes, then occupied himself in a conversation with a worshipper. I let it go, thinking that I couldn't alone fight the nasty perception of me and *Ammi* that Abbu's family had built for us.

Financial troubles were also gathering over our heads like thick black clouds.

"Listen, you must get employed immediately. Our condition may not be good in the upcoming days," *Ammi* said to me, seated on her Janamaz (prayer mat). I swallowed audibly, still thinking about Abbu's first marriage. My mind was flipping back and forth, and I somehow mustered up the courage to put forth the most spine-chilling question to her.

"*Ammi,* do you know anything about Abbu's first marriage?"

Ammi's face turned pale as if I was going to relinquish my religion. "Who told you this?" *Ammi* asked, flummoxed.

"Dadi," I said.

"Did she tell you? Really?"

"I overheard them talk about it," I replied. *Ammi* turned to look at the front door, hoping for a distraction to walk in. "*Ammi,* why did you keep it a secret?"

"Leave it! Not everything can be shared with the kids," she protested.

"Why?" I pressed further.

"I feel sorry for it. Also, it was his past," *Ammi* said. "How long ago was it? Why did it dissolve?" I put a flurry of questions to her.

Finally, *Ammi* sighed and started, "It happened before our marriage. It had lasted only for seven months. As per your Dadi's remarks, your Abbu's first wife was someone called Nasreen begum and she was mentally retarded."

"So, Abbu divorced her?" I asked, biting the skin under my nails

"Yes."

I wondered why it had taken him seven months to realise that she was mentally unwell. "What all do you know about her?" I prodded further.

"That's it. I never asked your Abbu about it," she said, taking a sip of water. She further instructed me not to enquire about it anymore, since it was a matter of distant past. I waited for her to say more, but she didn't.

Two months passed by since Abbu had left home. We led our lives in peace and quiet. None of our relatives bothered to check in on us. The yearning in *Ammi*'s eyes for me to get some employment made me cringe. I called up Gaurav again, who stood true to his words and gave me my old job back. This time, however, no room was left in my heart for Sneha, since the concern for my family had taken over.

The Other Marriage

We were struggling, stumbling, and staggering in our daily life, but Abbu and the relatives could not be bothered. Rest of the world had turned a deaf ear to our pleas. It had been a while since Abbu last gave *Ammi* Rs. 4,200 to meet the monthly expenses. Feasts were being hosted by my uncles for their children's marriages where Abbu participated wholeheartedly, not caring the least for his own family. I felt alone and helpless in my situation.

One day, Saif called home on landline and hurriedly said, "Hello bhai, can you come down to Khalil Street please? Now!"

"Why? What happened?" I asked curiously.

"Tahir and his brothers are after me, whipping me with their belts." Saif said, panting. My eyes bulged out at every word he said.

"Why the fuck are they doing that? Did you mess with them?" I asked furiously.

He paused and said, "No, never. One of them was staring at me, then the rest pounced at me all together. I couldn't escape. Please, come quickly." he said and hung up.

This street was only five minutes away from home. I narrated all this to *Ammi*. "Yes, go quickly and see what the matter is," *Ammi* said, chanting *Allah-o-Akbar*.

I was just about to enter through the main gate when I saw Saif walking out. His face shone more red than vermillion. I stepped up to see if our cousins were still around.

"Where're they?" I screamed at the on-lookers who had gathered to take pleasure in watching the tussle. Saif was sobbing uncontrollably in front of them.

"I'm going to fuck them all." My words escaped my mouth spontaneously.

"Tahir, Abdur Rehman, Asad and Inayat were all waiting for Saif. They attacked him as soon as he came out of the mosque," a child apprised me.

"Abdur Rehman? What? Are you sure?" I asked, baffled.

"Yes, he was also involved, that fucker!" Saif replied. I was deeply astonished as Abdur Rehman had once been my student. He had been one of my most respectful learners. Although, he was a son of Abbu's uncle. Despite everything, I had full faith in this family that at least they won't change their tune towards us. My jaw throbbed and my eyes grew blood-shot. I managed to escort Saif back home. When *Ammi* saw his wounded countenance, she cursed the assailants and fed Saif with her own hands. Saif's tears were intolerable for her, as she always showered more love over him than the rest of us.

"Please take rest and stop crying," *Ammi* consoled. I could see the terror and hatred in her eyes towards those abominable despicable boys. I assumed they were now resting in their palatial bungalows, with not even a tinge of guilt in them. Once again, we exercised patience and endurance we had inherited from *Ammi*.

"They have outnumbered us. That is why they have grown so audacious," I told *Ammi*. In totality, I had twenty-nine cousins. Their social connections went all the way up to the most influential politicians in Delhi and U.P. Many renowned lawyers bent down to them too. We, on the other end, had no such high reaching acquaintances.

"Stop thinking about them. Carve out your own career and they will all get bogged down by your success. Even if you are required to slog your guts out in that direction, you've got to do it. Ignore the rest," *Ammi* said, dabbing at Saif's bruises with her dupatta.

There were three things that continuously buzzed in my mind. One, Abbu's first marriage; two, why *Ammi* never said anything against Abbu's brutalities; three, why Abbu trusted his brothers over everybody else.

Ammi and all my siblings turned in at midnight, but I couldn't get even a wink of sleep all the way up to Fajar Namaz (dawn prayer). I got up and went to the mosque, my head spinning and my eyes sore. I felt so fed up with my harried cousins that I felt like I could kill them. I didn't even pay heed to the Imam sahab's preaching that day. Subconsciously, I copied the people around me. I just couldn't meditate. Something told me, "You have got to be strong now. After your *Ammi*, you'll be the most significant one in your family. If you fall weak, all your siblings will be in hot water." I had resolved to be stronger, but didn't know the right path to pursue.

At daybreak, I stepped out to visit G-Tec. It was what *Ammi* had wanted me to do for a long time, and the crippling circumstances now necessitated it. My cousins, Tahir and Abdur Rahman, looked at me from the corner of the street. I stopped and leaned forward, looking straight into their eyes. "Come on, hit me! You sons of bitches!" I mumbled.

They whispered something among themselves. I unbuckled my belt and pulled it out to have something in my hand to combat. They didn't move an inch, neither did I. However, the images of my *Ammi* and siblings flashed across my mind and I decided to move on. These boys were not in the middle of a financial crisis like me, I realized, and decided to let it go. I boarded a bus to Kamla Nagar.

Sitting across the table from Gaurav, I put across the idea to him to start regular English classes. I had already persuaded all my students for it.

"Sir, it's a good idea," Gaurav said. "Initially, I might not be able to pay you for these classes, but based upon your performance and the response from students, I will proactively start paying," he added, fidgeting with a ball pen.

I had to prove my mettle, I figured. "No problem.

Sounds good," I said, flicking my hair.

While returning from there, my eyes invariably searched for boards of advocates and political representatives. I let my mind delve into fantasies of punching Tahir and Abdur Rahman in their jaws. I also envisioned filing a suit against all my bastard relatives, including Abbu.

Right behind Hansraj College, I found a white flex hanging on the gate of a bungalow that read, *RK Advocates & Solicitors.* Happiness surged though me like a wave and I entered. An office boy warmly welcomed me and offered me a glass of water.

"*Vakeel sahab* has gone out of town for some important work," he revealed.

"Can I speak with someone else, right now?" I grunted. The poor man must have noticed the frustration in my voice..

"Sir, ma'am should be reaching here any minute now. Please wait for a while," he said, perhaps feeling terrorized.

I read *ma'am*'s credentials outside her chambers, *Mrs. Monika Kharbanda–M.A, LLB.* I killed time skimming through newspapers till she arrived, which was after lunch, around 2.30 PM.

"Hi," I greeted her, standing up.

"Keep sitting, please," she said, smiling.

Without wasting another second, I shared with her the issues at home. She actively listened to me without any interruptions, nodding and acknowledging all that I said. At the end, she concluded, "Everything is possible in the light of law. Your case is worth giving attention," she sympathised. I sighed in relief. She claimed that she had never come across such an unbelievable dispute. Abbu's misdoings had baffled even a lawyer.

"Look Zaidan, you will need to pay some fee. Only then can this matter be dealt with. We will dispense justice for you," she said matter of factly without taking a pause.

Her words disillusioned me of her seemingly selfless approach. "I'm not in a position to pay any amount," I said, seeking some polite response from her.

"Brother, it's impossible. Your case will include drafting, filing and hearing. It all takes time and impeccable proceeding," she elaborated.

"Ma'am, I humbly beseech you to have mercy on me," I said, growing tearful.

"Look, we're like a PCO. You can't make a call until you drop a coin," she said, mimicking the action with her fingers. I left the place disheartened and boarded bus no. 212 to get back home.

Saif was recovering from his injuries and was now able to walk straight. His wounds had been minor, but had left an everlasting mark on me. I shared my interaction with the lawyer with *Ammi*.

"I wish we had some affiliation with politicians, judges or policemen. They would have been of great help, for sure," I said aloud.

Ammi stopped doing her chores, sat down in front of me and said, "You may talk to anybody in the world, but the greatest help always comes from Allah. He brings all grief and joy. Mark my words!"

"But *Ammi*, one ought to have links with such people." I retorted.

"Leave it. Allah is the greatest of all." Nazia said, moving across the room.

Things had gotten gloomier than before, and my vindictive nature did not help. I prayed to the Almighty everyday that he would turn the tables on our enemies. As the Islamic scholars at the Madrasa had taught me, I had unshakable belief in Allah, yet the situation had filled me with chagrin.

"Don't offer your prayers at the Fakhruddin Mosque. It's not safe," *Ammi* instructed Saif. This was the place where Saif had been attacked. Most of my uncles and relatives lived near that mosque.

"Rarely do I go there," Saif said angrily. I knew that he had been in a lot of pain unnecessarily, so his frustration was justified.

"When you go out, get some eggs. I will make an omelet for Saif," *Ammi* said, looking at me.

"Yes, I'm going now," I said, slipped into my chappals and left.

A popular egg wholesaler used to set up shop near our house. A huge number of customers thronged his establishment from dawn to dusk, since his prices were cheaper than the rest. When I reached there, I saw Shamim bhai there. He had come to buy a dozen trays to sell at his shop to his retail customers.

"Asslamualikum," I greeted him. He reciprocated and seemed interested in striking a conversation with me.

"How's Saif doing now?" he asked.

"How do you know about it?" I retorted, narrowing my eyes in suspicion. He went on to tell me how news of the incident had spread like wildfire. I had goosebumps, and Shamim bhai noticed it. "Why did they do so? They've all been Saif's friends in the past." I said, almost complaining.

"I will tell you something, but please don't reveal it to anyone else," he said, lowering his voice in a way quintessential of himself. I leaned in closer. "They didn't intend to hit Saif," he started. "It's your father who instigated them. They discussed the entire matter at my shop. I heard it all. Your father is going to turn even more of your relatives against you and your family. Stay cautious!" he said in a single breath.

"What does Abbu want?" I asked, snorting.

"Well, maybe a second marriage," he said, stiffening his lips.

"Uncle, it's already his second marriage," I corrected him.

"What do you mean?" he asked.

"He was married once before *Ammi*. Dadi got that woman divorced in just seven months. Don't you know at all?" I asked, raising my voice.

"Goodness me," he sighed.

I realized that most people were unaware of Abbu's first marriage. It had been kept a major secret. I wondered how the whole family had been protecting this unbelievable mystery. Shamim bhai suggested that I go speak to Irfan uncle–Abbu's eldest brother. Not only was Abbu very obedient to him, he was also the wealthiest of all his brothers, and hence the most respected. He owned a three storey house in Mohalla, Kishan Ganj. I had met him multiple times and he appreciated my academic achievements. He used to tell everybody about me, "My nephew speaks very impressive English. He is a learned man." Like most people in our economic and social strata, he believed that an English speaking person could conquer anything.

Owing to the respect he commanded, he was also obnoxiously selfish, ruthless and brutal. He could kill for money. He had offered seven Haj (pilgrimage to Makah and Medina), yet I had never heard of a good deed from him. He was a powerful patriarch of the family and I decided to approach him and request his immediate intervention in the matter.

Before I proceeded with it however, I decided to get *Ammi*'s counsel on the matter. I rushed back home and shared my thoughts with her. Surprisingly, she agreed. "He has been a sound decision maker in the past," she said. I was delighted and relieved.

I went to their house that very night to get a chance to talk to him before he slept. His youngest son Mohd. Ahmed welcomed me in and led me to Irfan Uncle. I greeted them all warmly. At once, he asked Mohd. Ahmed to get CocaCola for me. The minute I began my story, he lit a Red&White cigarette and started smoking. I had a feeling that he already knew the entire matter. He only pretended to listen and avoided eye contact with me. Perhaps, someone from Abbu's side had already come and told him their side of the story. I didn't touch the tall glass of CocaCola in front of me. At the end, he simply asked, "Why did you not try to retain your Abbu when he decided to go away?"

I felt helpless. "I have come to you because we can't see any other viable option to deal with this," I said, gazing at tantalising bubbles rising up in the glass in front of me.

"I know, my son," he said, dropping the ash off his cigarette.

I couldn't know if he had been told everything. "I beseech you to look into it. We're terribly disturbed," I said with folded hands.

"Everything will be all right," he consoled me, smiling.

I came back home and shared the same with *Ammi*. "Allah is the greatest of all," she said, sighing. Her faith was infallible, but I was desperately looking for an instant miracle.

The following day, I had some interviews scheduled at some BPO consultancies. I left home as per the schedule, freeing my mind of all the negative vibes I had been living with. As I waited at the bus stop for bus

#721, I caught sight of Mohd. Ahmed, Tahir and Rizwan uncle walking toward me. As the equation between us had now changed, I bypassed the customary greetings. Many buses came and went, but #721 was nowhere in sight. They stopped next to me, frowning and grunting.

Tahir, the one who had orchestrated Saif's harassment, stepped forward and said, "What would you do if I hit you with this?" He pulled out a hockey stick from his kurta.

"What if I hit you back?" I retorted with a stare.

Tahir's eyes popped out and he shook his head.

"You, bastard!" Mohd. Ahmed abused. "Fuck him!" Tahir waged. That was their cue as they started slapping and hitting me with the hockey stick and beer bottles they had picked up from the road-side.

Two passers-by came to rescue me. "What's happening? He's all alone," they yelled.

"He fucking beats his father," Rizwan uncle lied. Mohd. Ahmed held me by my collar, while Tahir kept striking my knees with the hockey stick and Rizwan uncle ceaselessly slapped me across me face and ears.

A huge crowd gathered around. "Leave him, for God's sake," an old man shouted. Mohd. Ahmed pushed me back and they all vanished. That old man offered me his hand to help me stand up. I felt terribly ashamed amidst so many people hovering over me. Somebody got me my spectacles back. I looked down at myself. My jeans were ridden with dust, two buttons of my T-shirt were missing, and a lot of my hair had been plucked out in the struggle. Despite the bruises, I didn't see any open wounds, nor was there blood anywhere. I sighed heavily and thanked Allah. It took me a while to realise, however, that I couldn't hear from my right ear.

All the way from the bus stop to my house, I kept rubbing my ear and rolled my little finger in it, but all was in vain. When I reached home, *Ammi* avoided making eye contact with me. She covered her face with her scarf and went on reciting the holy Quran. I pulled the scarf away from her face, and she began to weep. I got a lump in my throat. Saif had barely convalesced yet, and I came back home with fresh wounds on my body. "I had a terribly uneasy feeling about an hour ago," she told me. She had known.

When I told her about the pain in my ear, she got an eardrop from the other room and administered it. I lay down and closed my eyes, trying to erase from my mind the trauma I had just been through. Despite all our effort, my ear did not get better. *Ammi's* frustration at my condition and the condition in general made her lost her cool. She turned red with rage, pulled out her sharpest knife and stormed towards the main gate with an intention to slay if she would find the men who did this to her children. I had never seen her look so revengeful. I did not want to stop her, but Nazia intervened.

"*Ammi*, they only want to provoke us to do something stupid. We don't have enough money to demand justice at police stations or courts," said Nazia, holding *Ammi*'s hand. "We need to avoid them like the plague. Our days shall change, inshallah."

"Inshallah," Saif echoed.

I felt too beaten down to say or do anything. Nazia was correct, we were helpless. *Ammi* returned, but her anger did not subside.

The next day, *Ammi* asked, "How's your ear now?" "It's better, alhamdulillah," I lied, tilting my head. "When will our days get better?" Saif asked frustratedly.

"Thank the Almighty. You're young and healthy, Mash Allah," *Ammi* said.

"*Ammi*, don't console me with all this," Saif protested.

"Yes, he's right," I supported him.

"Shall we file an FIR?" Saif proposed.

"Don't even think about it. They're all bought for. Once you get entangled in a police case, it will become a life-long affair," she insisted.

"They say that the police is working at all times for our safety and comfort. If not us, who are they even working for?" Saif questioned irrationally.

"The big sharks," *Ammi* said. Saif sighed deeply.

Somebody knocked at the door just then. Nazia went to open it and let in Rizwan uncle and Majid Khan, Shama aunty's brother. "It felt like our miseries would never end. These men were absolutely shameless." *Ammi* said and went to the other room. Nazia let them in and offered them water. Every passing second was difficult to endure. I could see Rizwan uncle looking around for the rest of us.

"He's calling you," Nazia called out to *Ammi* after a few seconds. *Ammi* and I emerged from the other room. I went straight for the main door and locked it from the inside so that no more people could enter.

"Sit down, please. Majid, let them sit," Rizwan uncle said sarcastically. He didn't look at me, neither did Majid. Majid and I were of the same age and had shared some good times together in the past. Yet at this point of time, he ignored me. Having had a glass of water, Rizwan uncle cleared his throat. I had a premonition that a massive blow was coming our way. "Bhabi, can you give me your final answer?" he asked, still not looking at her.

"What answer?" *Ammi* asked, awestruck.

"Don't be innocent," he remarked rudely. "Do you want to live peacefully with Farooq bhai or not?" he asked. I felt like grabbing a dagger and impaling him with it.

"I've never had any issues with him," *Ammi* said solemnly.

"I don't want to listen to all this bullshit," he snubbed her. I shifted uncomfortably in my seat

"We are here to tell you that Farooq bhai has decided to go for another marriage," Rizwan uncle continued. All of us remained in our seats, motionless and absolutely stunned.

Thereafter, the two of them put on their footwear and left.

The Brutal Act Of Divorce

"Where can I see B.Com Pass results?" I enquired at the information window of the School of

Open Learning (SOL) center.

"It's already out. You may check it on the walls," an officer said, pointing towards the exit gate. I saw the list of results for various courses pasted on the walls. I scanned through the roll numbers for the initial alphabets of my name, but couldn't find my name there. I looked westwards, as the Muslim faith commands one to bow down in the direction of the setting sun, and though of Kaaba to do miracles for me. Simultaneously, I read some important verses from the Holy Quran.

"Excuse me, I can't find my name here," I said to a fellow student who was leaning against the wall. Already quite flustered, he gave me an annoyed look. I scanned the list again, moving my lips in a mumbled prayer.

My score was as follows:

1. Financial Accounting–44
2. Economics–36
3. Urdu–52
4. English–45

I was delighted for a moment, with the relief of having passed all the subjects. The marks reflected my capability. I added up the numbers and calculated my percentage. Those who said, 'There's no future for those scoring below 50%' terrified me.

"Hey, how much did you score?" a student whom I had met a couple of times before, asked.

I remained silent, and gestured to the wall. "I'm just a breath shy of 50%. Economics spoiled it for me. It's 49.5%," I said, pretending to be indifferent.

People were celebrating all around me, huddling with and hugging each other. I fisted my hands and kept walking, out to the bus stand. I had the urge to speak to *Ammi* immediately. While my life seemed to be falling apart, the world went on at its regular pace. Even the sky seemed heavy with the burden of clouds. As I boarded bus no. 212, a sinking feeling housed in my stomach. The bus conductor was playing old songs on the radio and an old passenger yelled, "Raise the volume." The general cheerfulness of the surrounding failed to make me feel any better though.

It had gotten dark by the time I reached home. I knew *Ammi* wouldn't understand that such a low percentage could paralyse my career forever, and the thought of facing her with this news made me cringe. I wished I had better news for her. She welcomed me in, smiling as usual.

"When are your B.Com results out?" she asked cheerfully, while engaged in her daily chores. I fought with the idea of revealing the result to her, though another part of me wanted to wait till I got a job.

Finally, I decided I couldn't keep it in me for too long. "Well, I haven't seen it yet, but one of my mates told me that I've successfully gotten through," I said, looking away from her.

"Oh, great! Have you passed in all the papers?" *Ammi* asked, visibly excited.

"Oh, yes!" I said, pleased to have made her happy. "Alhamdulillah, I'm so happy," *Ammi* said.

"You're a graduate now?" Nazia and Saif asked in unison and exchanged smiles. Nazia was the most excited, and couldn't wait to tell her friends that her brother was the first in their little community to have graduated. *Ammi* asked Saif to bring a kilo and a half of fresh chicken, so she could prepare a celebratory feast. She prepared delicious Korma that we relished down to the last bite. She then served 'kheer' for dessert. Nobody mentioned Abbu at all. My heart grew a little lighter amidst all the laughter and joy.

Nazia suggested that I should go for a job at an MNC. I imagined myself in smart trousers, rushing to office confidently.

"I know what you're thinking," Nazia remarked, smiling.

"What?"

"You will soon work in a plush office. But don't give up!" she said, dropping her eyes.

"May Allah bestow the best upon you!"

"Ameen!" I reciprocated. It was the best wishes of my family and the positivity they enveloped me in that kept me going.

After a while, there was a loud knock on the door again. Saif went to open it. "Who's there?" he called out, loud and irritated. We heard someone clearing their throat on the other side. I was in the washroom. All laughter and celebration ceased. We waited with bated breaths. Saif opened the door partially to look outside, then turned around, his mouth curled down in a grimace. "Abbu!" he whispered with a ominous tone.

We looked at each other in trepidation. Abbu had never taken interest in my academics before. Moreover, the popularity of my coaching always baffled him.

Abbu came in, wearing a green kurta and a white lungi. His skull cap seemed as if it was a part of his head. Dadi followed in after him. Nazia gasped and rushed to the other room. *Ammi* and Faiz got into another room. We didn't have any courage left for another confrontation.

"Come on, where've you gone to hide?" Abbu barked. "You bloody bitch!" he provoked *Ammi*. "Why've you created such a mess? I'll ruin you."

Abbu and I traded blank looks. *Ammi* didn't utter a word.

"This is very disrespectful," Dadi muttered, chewing on beetle nut.

Ammi stepped out, her face impassive. "As if I would ever be happy staying away from my husband," she said, not meeting their eyes.

"Look, how sharp her tongue is! She misbehaves with me all the time. Not only does she do it, but makes her sons do so too," Abbu fibbed. I remained standing quietly by the door. "What the fuck is going on between Majid and Nazia?" he asked finally. I couldn't believe his words. A father was casting aspersions at his own daughter. Nazia appeared before him, utterly shocked. Abbu reached for my old cricket bat lying in one corner of the room. I stepped in his way and tried to restrain him.

"What's this? Don't do this. Please, beat me if you want to," I said, and his lips twisted for some reason. Dadi made no effort to mitigate this nonsense.

"Arrey, why did you exchange a smile with Majid at Rubina's wedding?" Dadi asked Nazia. We had gone to attend the wedding of a distant relative the previous weekend. Since they were our common relatives, Abbu had been there too, and was now targeting his own daughter for a trivial gesture. Moreover, Majid had always been like a brother to all of us. He never visited our house because of Abbu.

"You slut!" Abbu snouted at *Ammi*. I got goose- bumps all over my skin. Nazia tried to retaliate, but I stopped her.

"See, this is what the kids here are upto," said Abbu, drawing Dadi's attention to his words. His atrocities upon us were unaccounted for. "I want a divorce now," Abbu yelped. *Ammi* and I were stunned to hear his words. Dadi still didn't utter a word.

The door was knocked again, and in came Irfan uncle along with his three sons, people who used to be my well-wishers. They towered over me and *Ammi*. When they were toddlers, they had rested and played in *Ammi*'s lap, but all had been forgotten now. I knew they hadn't brought any good news for us. *Ammi* veiled her face with her scarf as soon as they entered, as was the traditional protocol.

"Why don't you divorce Hajira?" spat Irfan uncle, frowning. Dadi and Abbu stayed mum.

"Please don't let this happen, uncle. We beg you," pleaded Nazia, but was ignored by all.

Abbu started recounting all the fights that had taken place in the last few months in his own flawed perspective. He went over and over about the same things. Irfan uncle and Dadi listened to him patiently.

"Bhai, I would like to talk to you for two minutes, please. Let me tell you the truth. You all have been under the wrong impression," *Ammi* pleaded with teary eyes. Irfan uncle thought for a moment, then agreed to listen. The door was knocked again and about a dozen of my paternal and maternal cousins landed at our house. *Ammi* remained indifferent to the new audience.

"Bhai, he has been in an extra marital relationship with Rashid the accountant's sister. He's been lying to us. I overheard their phone conversation," *Ammi* said, finally breaking her silence. Abbu's cheeks grew pale and beads of sweat formed over his brow. There was pin drop silence in the room for a while.

"All rubbish. I don't even know where she is," Abbu defended himself, avoiding an eye contact with any of us. Ironically, this explosive disclosure didn't come as a surprise to any of them. The fact that he said *'...where she is'* instead of *'...who she is'* irked me deeply.

"Can he not survive without another marriage?" *Ammi* sighed.

A part of me expected Irfan uncle to be sympathetic, however, he said, "Do you have any evidence of his relationship with that lady?" *Ammi* pointed to Abbu's Reliance cell-phone.

"It's gone out of order," Abbu said, swallowing audibly. Irfan uncle gestured to one of his sons to trace the call details.

"Any clue what the starting digits of her number are?" Irfan uncle asked *Ammi*.

"92-127," *Ammi* said, promptly enough. My cousins searched for the number in Abbu's phone, but to no success. Abbu snatched his phone back as soon as they were done.

"We can't do anything as long as the number is not confirmed. Is there anything else?" Irfan uncle asked *Ammi*.

"How do I know?" *Ammi* said meekly.

The door was knocked yet again. "Good God," I sighed. It was Dr. Abdul Kareem, a Qazi (Arabic scholar, magistrate of the Shariya court of law). All the men in the room reached for their skull caps and put them on. I felt extremely glad for his presence, for we had known each other for five years. I religiously offered the Namaz led by him, and had immense respect for him due to his doctorate degree in Islamic studies. He greeted everyone and cleared his throat before taking out a stack of papers to write on. "What do we need to do?" Dr. Kareem asked, looking at everyone.

"I honestly don't know what she wants out of me," Abbu said, agitated.

Still behind her veil, *Ammi* spoke, "Qazi sahab, I hope you understand this better. He got my son under black magic and occultism. Zaidan's head spun quite often and monkeys used to appear in his dreams. Sometimes, he saw pigs while sleeping."

Dr. Kareem smiled broadly at the description of my nightmares. "Pigs and monkeys are out of my comprehension," he said, writing down something in Arabic. *Ammi* further told him about consulting some black magic experts. Dr Kareem seemed reluctant to pay heed.

"Mr. Farooq, what would you like to say?" he asked with utmost politeness.

Dadi hissed something in Abbu's ear, surely some new scheme to swindle us. "What can I do or say?" Abbu started. "I've been pushed for everything, and remarriage is my last resort. I need a partner to look after me and my parents," Abbu said, gulping down a glass full of water.

"He casts aspersions on Nazia, his own daughter. I want to know if this is true fatherhood," *Ammi* exclaimed, sitting down.

Dadi screamed, " Stop it, please. My son can't live with you anymore." They all had come with a common intention to break the bond. Even Dr. Kareem was devoid of any judicial protection under the Sharia law. I continuously attempted to initiate a dialogue with him, but he avoided making eye contact with me.

"Hajira, will you live with him wherever he takes you?" asked Irfan uncle, pulling out a piece of paper from his pocket.

"Yes, of course! After all, he's my husband," *Ammi* said at once.

"I will keep her and the children in a rented house. This is my condition," Abbu said, adamant and illogical. I figured he wanted us out of this house, as he had been trying to do for months. Nobody questioned him on this.

Without discussing with us, *Ammi* said affirmatively, "Give me five minutes." Abbu and Irfan uncle went into the drawing room to deliberate. No one talked, not even mumbled anything.

The door was knocked yet again, and Tayyab and Rizwan uncle entered. They went straightaway into the drawing room where Irfan uncle and Abbu were seated. In the other room, *Ammi,* Nazia and I prayed to Allah for good fortune. About half an hour later, everyone assembled back in the room where Dr. Kareem was all set to take down all the facts of the matter.

"Look, our brother is not guilty at all. It's Hajira who has brought shame and frustration to the family," Tayyab uncle insisted. Dr. Kareem had no counter questions to this, but simply nodded instead. "All her allegations regarding black magic, an illicit relationship and other shit are absolutely fabricated," Tayyab uncle added.

"Why would a father do such things to his son? Why would he get into an illicit relationship after two decades of his marriage?" Dr. Kareem asked, scratching his salt & pepper beard. His words scared the hell out of me. An eminent Qazi from Dar-loom as him was arriving at a conclusion after heeding to only one party, the more powerful one too.

"You should leave them, Farooq bhai. We'll get you married again sooner than later," Tayyab uncle said, spitting his beetle into a spittoon.

"Yes, they will all turn paupers and be on the road soon," Dadi said, adding fuel to the fire.

"What do I do? My sons have beaten me on several occasions. It's too much! My wife makes them do it, and I feel highly insecure at home. Who knows, they might strangle me tomorrow," Abbu said, folding his handkerchief into a neat square.

A little later, Dr. Kareem asked, "What's your final decision?"

Abbu looked at all his nephews, brothers and then at Dadi. "Look, I can get twenty wives, but my brothers are more precious to me than anyone else," Abbu said. I jumped out of my skin at his words and saw *Ammi* and my siblings go wild with fear. Nazia was frozen in her spot.

Before either of us could say anything, Abbu pronounced, "Talaaq! Talaaq! Talaaq!"

It sent shivers down my spine. A deep silence prevailed in the courtyard where we stood, and pinched me sore. The ground beneath my feet seemed to have shifted. I gulped audibly and looked around. My uncles and cousins stood motionless, but unsurprised, Dr. Kareem looked unaffected, and Dadi's lips twitched up in the shadow of a smile, as if all this had been pre- planned and had now come to a successful execution. I wanted to shake them all by the shoulders and scream, but none of them tried to bring this terrifying ordeal to an end. *Ammi* stared at the sky in disbelief, her eyes welling up with tears of hopelessness. She didn't utter a word of resistance, much like the whole of her life upto this day. I would have given anything in that moment to bring her out of this heart-wrenching situation. I couldn't fathom whether my hatred for Abbu surpassed my infinite compassion towards *Ammi,* but I remained frozen in my spot. Nazia and Saif started sobbing quietly and went to stand by *Ammi*. A twenty-one year old marriage, and a family of five had been dissolved in less than three seconds.

***

It took us many days after that event to even come to terms with the fact that Abbu was no longer a part of our family. Despite his atrocities, he had been a part of this house, our daily lives and the delegate of our dignity and honour in the society we lived in. With him gone, we were reduced to a void, a thing to be shunned, an insult to our own existence. What's worse, it was for no fault of our own. *Ammi* had been the best wife a man could have, pious and subservient. Yet, such a fate had befallen us.

A week later, I consulted some other Qazis in the city regarding the matter. They all rebuked Dr. Kareem's actions saying that the Holy Quran didn't permit such a divorce. By protocol, he should've granted both of them a three months' period to let it settle mutually. One Talaaq a month should've been the right approach. I was in deep shock. Despite having known me for a long time, Dr. Kareem hadn't heard *Ammi*'s plea. Other scholars called him greedy and unscrupulous. I came to rely upon their opinion.

Later, a close friend of Dr. Kareem apprised me of his real nature. He shared an astounding fact that Dr. Kareem had charged Abbu with Rs. 50,000 for that one- sided Talaaq. I attempted to meet him several times, but he deliberately distanced himself from me. I told *Ammi* everything about his filthy practice, but she was un-moved. She seemed to have deeply internalised the barbarity done unto her. More than two decades of marriage and quietude had perhaps silenced the voice of her dissent. Even the religion of spirituality that she lived and breathed every second of her life had only brought her more suffering and solitude via the words of the corrupt Dr. Kareem.

She was in her *Iddat* period of three months and ten days. We were deprived of any share of Abbu's properties. Only the house was left to us, and a cheque of Rs. 9000 was sent by Abbu to *Ammi* for meeting her *Iddat* expenses. Mathematically, a hundred rupees per day was my *Ammi*'s compensation for all those years of cooperation, bearing his atrocities, and bringing up four children all on her own.

Abbu married Rashid's sister the very next month, while *Ammi* was still serving her *Iddat* period. He wore a finely stitched black suit on his Dawat-e-Walima, while *Ammi* wallowed in grief alone. There was nobody to comfort her though, not even my maternal uncles. They weren't even aware of this major setback in our life. Had my maternal grandfather been alive, he would've made some effort to prevent such a thing from happening. Our life was only getting tougher day by day, while none bothered to check in how we were getting along. I often contemplated suicide, but stopped myself at the thought of *Ammi* and my siblings.

"*Ammi*, these bloody bastards must be punished by Allah," I said furiously one day.

"Allah will do justice. Inshallah, we shall have better days. You must focus on building your career and never look back," *Ammi* consoled me. After a series of interviews, I got a customer care service job at Vodafone in Karol Bagh.

The Fake *Fatwa*

I started my *on job training* (OJT) at Vodafone in their swanky Karol Bagh office. I was one among a batch of twenty-five trainees who had come from Delhi and other states. Nitin, our mentor, told us on the first day that he would help us with our language and accent during the training period.

With all that was going on at home, I couldn't afford any distractions and diversions, but to focus on my work at hand and earn a handsome living for my family. Teaching English At G-Tec was never a long- term option for me, and *Ammi* was in favour of this decision.

I did not leave giving coaching altogether. From 8 PM to 10 PM everyday, I taught English to primary class students. I couldn't let go of any opportunity to earn money. Waves of revenge washed through me at the sight of my cousins driving swanky cars down my street. I could no longer relax.

In one of his sessions, Nitin said, "Success is the best revenge." It was exactly the kind of motivation I needed. He even counselled me on my English. I began to ape his style of speech. He spoke in a British accent, as he had lived there for almost a decade. I idealized him, in fact, most of us did. When I told him about my family's catastrophic story, he motivated me to bounce back and not lose hope. He shared with me a famous quote by Winston Churchill–*If you're going through hell, keep going.*

Indeed, my life was no less than hell. All my relatives had turned their backs on us, even those on my maternal side couldn't be bothered. Abbu was intoxicated on his new innings in life. His third marriage was no cause of guilt for him. His new wife was twenty years younger than he was. He took her to Nainital for their honeymoon, while *Ammi* hadn't even been fortunate enough to see the Red Fort.

Regardless, she remained unaffected by what anyone thought of us. Even though Abbu had brainwashed everyone against us, she told me, "Zaid, you needn't approach anyone. Time is a great healer." She despised me trying to clarify our stand to neighbours, relatives and strangers. She didn't want the matter to be shared publicly anymore than it had already been.

One day at work, Nitin spared fifteen minutes of his time to listen to me. "Of course, it is illegal and heart-rending, but you have to have patience," he said, lighting a cigarette in the smoking zone. "Show the world that you can lead your family all alone. Don't mess with them. They will compel you to do something immature, so they can harass you even more."

"Sir, all of this feels like a cruel joke. He even accused me and my siblings of beating him and chastised Nazia for having love affairs," I said.

Nitin was flabbergasted. "May I ask you a question?" he asked in a serious tone.

"Go ahead, please," I said anxiously.

"Is your mother happy?" Nitin asked, his cigarette wedged between his fingers.

"How could she be? She never expressed her grief to us, but it's the greatest loss for her," I replied.

"Brother, never leave her alone," he said, and I nodded.

Nitin was my only support and counsel outside of home. He even helped me purchase grammar books and guided me through the studying process. Only nine out of twenty-five trainees made it to the production floor after the training, and I was one of them. I couldn't believe that a Madrasa educated guy was being recognized such in the mainstream corporate world. *Ammi* was the happiest upon hearing this news, almost as if she had regained everything.

Days rolled by without granting much relief, until I came to hear of an Islamic scholar Maulana Aslam Qadiri based in west Nizamuddin, New Delhi. Despite having been cheated by Dr. Kareem, I felt gravitated to wards Maulana Aslam Qadiri. Many people spoke to me about him and his unparalleled wisdom.

At the local mosque one day, I asked a fellow believer, "What do you think of Maulana Aslam Qadiri? Is he an uncorrupt scholar?" The guy looked at me in great shock. Perhaps the word 'uncorrupt' had jolted him. The entire Muslim community blindly believed in such scholars without a hint of critical discernment or dissension.

"We're not allowed to criticise a scholar, brother. They've gained all the knowledge of God," he retorted rapidly.

"But all of them are not absolutely right," I said assertively, and shared *Ammi*'s agony with him. "That bastard Dr. Kareem played an instrumental role in this," I stressed. "And he did all of this for a price of Rs. 50,000."

The man uncapped his head and looked at me distraught. "A burnt hand dreads fire," I said in a repulsive manner.

He empathised with me and told me what he knew about Maulana Aslam Qadiri. I found out that he was in his nineties and held an honorific position as an Islamic scholar and peace activist. He was known for having translated the Holy Quran into contemporary English, and for writing a commentary on the Quran. He had authored a book called *The quotes of the Prophet Muhammad S.A.W.* His televised lectures have appeared on various popular TV networks. He had also received the Demiurgus Peace International Award under the patronage of the former Soviet President Mikhail Gorbachev, as well as India's third-highest civilian honor–the Padma Bhushan in January, 2000.

I grew curious to meet Maulana, and share with him the predicament of my family. "How can I meet the Maulana?" I asked the man.

"He holds sermons at Nizamuddin every Sunday. You can meet him there in person. He's highly educated and delivers all his talks in English," the man told me, patting my back. "Go to his peace center this weekend. I will accompany you, if you wish," he added graciously. He was the first person after a long time who had shown a positive supporting interest in the matter of my family's troubles.

The coming Sunday, I set off for the Peace Center. I sat amongst a huge crowd of listeners who had come to attend his sermon. He arrived wearing a black turban and an Arabian-Islamic white gown that hung down to his ankles. He briefly talked about the Islamic tenets, but greatly emphasised upon the harmony and affection amongst all sects and believers. He didn't just thumbed his prayer beads and recited the holy Quran

Meaninglessly. He was dignified and rightly glorified in his translations and deep interpretations of the Holy Quran.

"Allah is the Almighty God for all, not just Muslims," Maulana said, standing at the stage. His words sent chills down my spine.

"Is it possible to meet him in person?" I asked a visitor.

He barely heard me at first, his attention completely focused on the Maulana. "Well, I've tried it several times, but in vain," he said and chuckled.

"Oh God, please grant me a chance to share my agony with him," I prayed. As soon as Maulana winded up his sermon for the day, I sprang up from my seat and chased after him. Some of his attendants tried to stop me, but I pleaded with them, "Let me just meet him for five minutes, please."

Perhaps it was my day, for the servants let me proceed with a warning to make it quick.

"Mashallah! Mashallah! Mashallah!" said the Maulana smiling as I approached him. His face exuded a divine light. He carried a neat and clean demeanour, and wore musk attar that fragranced the air around him.

"Hazrat, my *Ammi* got divorced recently. I doubt that it has not been discharged in accordance with the Islamic jurisprudence," I said, out of breath.

"Catch your breath first, son. May I see the *Talaq Nama* (Divorce Papers)?"

I took them out of my bag and handed them to him. He flipped through the papers while one of his servants combed his thick long beard.

"Who's this demon?" he screamed wrathfully. "How can a divorce be based on such silly reasons?" His face scrunched up in anger. "Call Dr. Kareem right away," he commanded. Dr. Kareem's number was mentioned at the bottom of the divorce papers. They dialled him thrice, but he did not answer. When he picked up on the fourth attempt, Maulana asked him directly, "On what basis have you written this divorce?"

"Who're you?" Dr. Kareem asked snobbishly.

"I am calling from the Peace Center at Nizamuddin," Maulana replied.

"Well, I can't disclose any information on this matter, and please don't call me again. I have a very busy schedule," Dr. Kareem said in a condescending manner.

"I'm from Deoband Madarsa and so are you. Don't defame such a prestigious institution for the sake of some hefty cheese, for God's sake!" Maulana thundered.

"Mind your own business," said Dr. Kareem and disconnected the call.

Maulana sighed and turned back to me. "Son, this is heart-rending indeed. Allah doesn't like Talaaq. Particularly, one of this sort. Lured by money, scholars like Dr. Kareem issue such *Fatwas*. Instances like this bring a bad name to our community and religion, and we're cursed by the society for it," he said, placing his hand on my shoulder.

"What shall I do now?" I asked, expecting a miracle. "Well, all is done now. He bears the Qasmi stamp (a stamp of religious authority awarded by the Deoband

Madarsa). People will comply by its authority," he said dejectedly.

"Allah hafiz," his servants intercepted and escorted me out.

About The Author

Mohd. Faizan (M.A. (English), MBA & LLB)

Mohd. Faizan was born in an Islamic scholar's family in Delhi, and is hugely inspired by his mother– Rehnuma Khatoon. She has always been a driving force for him to pen down his pathos.

Providentially, Faizan has added many feathers to his cap, as he is professionally a Lawyer (Criminal & Arbitration), motivational speaker and an English language trainer. To his credit, he's been a corporate trainer for 9 years, contributing to RBS Business Services Pvt. Ltd. & Genpact International.

He harbours a keen interest in literature and passion for poetry that quenches his thirst for words weaved into multifarious yet soulful shades. He's a die-hard fan of Wordsworth's and Keats' poetry. Mark Twain & Allama Iqbal have had a great influence on him. He likes to interact with people from different walks of life to draw food for thought. Resultantly, his two poems

– *Those Were The Days* and *Those Blissful Eyes* have been published in International Anthologies: The Essence Of Eternal Happiness and Resonance respectively.

'The Sin of Omission' is only the first volume of a two part series. The author is currently working towards finishing the second title.

Facebook: mohd.faizan.942145

Email: faiziv3@yahoo.com

Twitter: @mdfaizanchaudh1

Method of divorce laid down in the Quran :

Whether the demand for divorce emanates from the husband or the wife, the method of divorce will be the one laid down in the Quran which is as follows:

Appoint an arbitrator

[Quran 4:35]: If a couple fears separation, you shall appoint an arbitrator from his family and an arbitrator from her family; if they decide to reconcile, God will help them get together. God is omniscient, cognizant.

Wait 4 months cooling off before divorce

[Quran 2:226 -227]: Those who intend to divorce their wives shall wait four months (cooling off), if they change their minds and reconcile, then God is Forgiver, Merciful. If they go through with the divorce, then God is Hearer, Knower.

If the estranged couple chooses separation, there must be two equitable witnesses to witness the divorce before God.

Alimony For widows and Divorcees

[Quran 2:240]: Those who die and leave wives, a WILL shall provide their wives with support for a year, provided they stay within the same household. If they leave, you commit no sin by letting them do whatever they wish, so long as righteousness is maintained. God is Almighty, Most wise.

[Quran 2:241]: The divorcees also shall be provided for, equitably. This is a duty upon the righteous.

Divorced women entitled to stay in the same house she stayed before divorce

[Quran 2:231]: If you divorce the women, once they fulfill their interim (three menstruations), you shall allow them to live in the same home amicably, or let them leave amicably. Do not take God's revelations in vain, Remember God's blessings upon you, and that He sent down to you the scripture and wisdom to enlighten you. You shall observe God, and know that God is aware of all things.

[Quran 2:229]: It is not lawful for the husband to take anything he had given her".

STEP 1

As a first step, when there is a marital discord, the husband/ wife will reason out with each other through discussions.

STEP 2

If differences persist. Then as a next step, the parties are asked to sexually distance themselves from each other in the hope that this temporary physical separation may encourage them to unite.

STEP 3

And if even this fails, they will once again discuss the seriousness of the situation and try to bring about reconciliation.

STEP 4

If the dispute still remains unresolved, as a fourth step, the parties to the dispute must place their matter before two arbitrators nominated by the family, one from the family of each spouse, for resolution.

It is only after the failure of the aforementioned four attempts at reconciliation that the first talaq is to be declared by the party initiating the divorce in the presence of two witnesses and the arbitrators. This declaration of divorce is to be followed by a waiting period called the *iddah.* Not more than two divorces can be pronounces within this period, the duration of which is three monthly courses.

For women who have attained menopause or suffer from amenorrhea the period of *iddah* is three months, and in the case of pregnant women it is till the termination of pregnancy.

And if the parties are unable to unite during *iddah,* the final irrevocable talaq can be pronounced by the party which initiated the divorce proceedings, but only after the expiry of the *iddah*. Once the final talaq has been invoked the marital bond is severed and the parties cease to be of any relation to each other.

All decisions taken before the witnesses and arbitrators must be recorded. The final divorce at the end of *iddah* must also be recorded in a *Talaaknama* by the arbitrators. The rights of the women on divorce must be safeguarded by the arbitrators and must be mentioned in the *talaaknama.*

Original copies of the same must be provided to both the parties.

IN THE SUPREME COURT OF INDIA Original Civil Jurisdiction Writ Petition (C) No. 118 of 2016 Shayara Bano … Petitioner versus Union of India and others … Respondents with Suo Motu Writ (C) No. 2 of 2015 In Re: Muslim Women's Quest For Equality versus Jamiat Ulma-I-Hind Writ Petition(C) No. 288 of 2016 Aafreen Rehman … Petitioner versus Union of India and others … Respondents Writ Petition(C) No. 327 of 2016 Gulshan Parveen … PetitionerUnion of India and others … Respondents Writ Petition(C) No. 665 of 2016 Ishrat Jahan … Petitioner versus Union of India and others … Respondents Writ Petition(C) No. 43 of 2017 Atiya Sabri … Petitioner versus Union of India and others … Respondents

JUDGMENT, Supreme of court of India

The petitioner's marital discord, and the petitioner's prayers: 1. The petitioner-Shayara Bano, has approached this Court, for assailing the divorce pronounced by her husband – Rizwan Ahmad on 10.10.2015, wherein he affirmed "... in the presence of witnesses saying that I gave 'talak, talak, talak', hence like this I divorce from you from my wife. From this date there is no relation of husband and wife. From today I am 'haraam', and I have become 'naamharram'. In future you are free for using your life ...". The aforesaid divorce was pronounced before Mohammed Yaseen (son of Abdul Majeed) and Ayaaz Ahmad (son of Ityaz Hussain) – the two witnesses. The petitioner has sought a declaration, that the 'talaq-ebiddat' pronounced by her husband on 10.10.2015 be declared as void ab initio. It is also her contention, that such a divorce which abruptly, unilaterally and irrevocably terminates the ties of matrimony, purportedlyunder Section 2 of the Muslim Personal Law (Shariat) Application Act, 1937 (hereinafter referred to as, the Shariat Act), be declared unconstitutional. During the course of hearing, it was submitted, that the 'talaq-e-biddat' (-triple talaq), pronounced by her husband is not valid, as it is not a part of 'Shariat' (Muslim 'personal law'). It is also the petitioner's case, that divorce of the instant nature, cannot be treated as "rule of decision" under the Shariat Act. It was also submitted, that the practice of 'talaq-e-biddat' is violative of the fundamental rights guaranteed to citizens in India, under 4 Articles 14, 15 and 21 of the Constitution. It is also the petitioner's case, that the practice of 'talaq-e-biddat' cannot be protected under the rights granted to religious denominations (-or any sections thereof) under Articles 25(1), 26(b) and 29 of the Constitution. It was submitted, that the practice of 'talaq-e-biddat' is denounced internationally, and further, a large number of Muslim theocratic countries, have forbidden the practice of 'talaq-ebiddat', and as such, the same cannot be considered sacrosanctal to thetenets of the Muslim religion.